INFLUENCE

PERSUADE

and WIN

INFLUENCE PERSUADE
and WIN

Build rapport with difficult
people and negotiate win-win
outcomes

96 POWERFUL WAYS
TO PERSUADE

Vince DaCosta

Vince DaCosta & Associates Inc.
Training Division
Toronto, Canada.

Canadian Cataloguing in Publication Data
Copyright © 1993 by Vince DaCosta
2nd printing . . . . December 1999

Vince DaCosta & Associates Inc.
Training Division
17 Ferrah St.
Unionville, Ontario,
Canada.   L3R 1N4

DaCosta, Vince, date
Influence, Persuade and Win
ISBN 0-9696564-0-8
1. Success in business. 2. Persuasion(Psychology).
3. Negotiation. 4. Interpersonal relations.
I. Title

HF5386.D22 1992   650.1'3   C92-095273-9
Published by:
Vince DaCosta & Associates Inc.
Training Division
17 Ferrah St.
Unionville, Ontario, Canada
L3R 1N4

                              Printed in Canada
                              by Webcom Ltd.

Acknowledgements

This book would never have been written but for the help and influence of many people:

My mother and father who instilled in me the values and attitudes I have lived by most of my life. I learned from them that honesty and integrity are not negotiable.

My old college principal David Davis who taught us that school was not to memorize Latin verbs, but to learn how to think.

Ken, Keith, George, Hyacinth, Hazel, Jean, Beulah and Mary, who were part of my world in the years before adulthood. I thank you all for your caring and companionship.

I thank my wife Hyacinth, for her painstaking care in reading, correcting and formatting all the pages of this book. For her ideas and suggestions for improving its quality. But most of all, for the final title: **Influence, Persuade and Win.**

I thank Jane Watson for her careful and thoughtful editing, and for her patience in deleting "that," which I use too frequently. Albert Lau for the Chinese lettering, Vince Fera for the behavioural style graphics and my associate Marcello Scarsella for his contribution as a sounding board for my ideas.

I thank my friends and colleagues from the two great organizations I belong to - Toastmasters International and National Speakers Association - for their encouragement and support. Peter Bender who kept prodding me to get it done. Reva Nelson who helped with the title. Susan Duxter, Kai Rambow, Tom Stoyan, Gerry Robert and Ron Ross who gave me advice when I needed it.

To all of you I say, thank you for the experiences you shared and the lessons you taught me.

- Vince DaCosta

To my wife Hyacinth
and our two daughters
Rosalie and Sheila

CONTENTS

Introduction

Chapter 1   *1*
A Win-Win Strategy for Reaching
Agreement

Chapter 2   *9*
The Critical Factor for Successful
Negotiating

Chapter 3   *17*
Modify Your Personal Style and Get the
Results You Want

Chapter 4   *37*
19 Strategies that Build Rapport,
Create a Positive Impact and Reduce
Tension

Chapter 5   *71*
18 Keys to Listening that Strengthen
Relationships and Build Trust

Chapter 6   *99*
12 Ways to Deal with Difficult People
and Negotiate Win-Win Outcomes

Chapter 7   *137*
21 Strategies for Successful Everyday
Negotiation

Chapter 8   *171*
16 Secrets for Presentations
that Give You Visibility and Credibility

Chapter 9   *201*
10 Ways to Increase Self-Worth,
Personal Confidence, Serenity and
Real Success

Chapter 10   *225*
The Art of Managing Success

INTRODUCTION

Persuasion is the creating of a positive climate where new thoughts begin to grow. It is the building of an environment where people listen and think and make changes in their behaviour. That change in behaviour is the result of a strong foundation of trust, confidence, respect and faith. How to build this climate and develop this trust is what this book is all about.

A hostile climate destroys growth. Plants, animals, initiative, creativity begin to wither and die when faced with hostile conditions. Sometimes we wonder why we have to force and cajole and pressure people into doing the things we want them to do. The answer is simple. We have failed to create the kind of climate that sponsors cooperation and motivation.

This book will show you how to negotiate win-win outcomes. It will introduce you to actions and strategies that win the confidence and respect of others. It will help you to build receptive climates and prompt closed minds to open. In short, it will show you how to **Influence, Persuade and Win.**

Vince DaCosta
Toronto, Canada

Chapter 1

A WIN-WIN STRATEGY
FOR REACHING AGREEMENT

Janet Somers went back to her neighbourhood car dealer's office for the third time in three months. She had purchased her new car about nine months before, using most of her hard-earned savings. The car ran well for a while, then started to stall in traffic. She brought it back for service but became disappointed and frustrated, as the car just kept on stalling.

Today she is upset, particularly since she narrowly avoided having an accident when the car stalled in traffic yesterday. "I'm really upset and disappointed at your service here," she says to the service manager, "This is the third time that I have had my car back for service. It's quite evident to me that nothing has been done." The service manager is cold and impassive and advises her there will be a charge this time. "Your warranty expired three days ago," he explains.

Janet is astonished. "But it was under warranty when the problem started," she retorts. "Yes, but your warranty has expired, and my hands are tied. It's company policy." Janet feels frustrated and angry. She feels helpless and looks around not knowing what to do. The service manager is silent and inflexible. Janet senses his negative attitude and feels she has no choice but to give in. She reluctantly authorizes the work to go ahead.

That night she berates herself for her lack of negotiating techniques and her weakness in the face of a stubborn and unreasonable service manager. She consoles herself that next time she will do better, but Janet probably knows that next time will be the same. She just is not a good negotiator.

Janet's experience is a good example of a win-lose outcome in a conflict situation. The service manager won, Janet lost!

The win-lose outcome

Resolving conflict or negotiating agreement is the process of satisfying needs. Your interests conflict with the needs of others, and you look for a way to work out an agreement that will satisfy both parties. If we were to represent the service manager's needs with a circle and Janet's needs by another circle, the conflict or disagreement might look something like this:

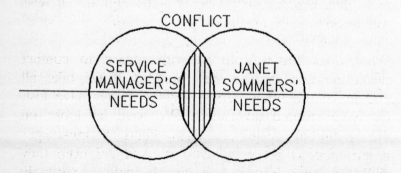

Janet's needs are infringing on the service manager's needs and a process of negotiation must take place to release the tension and diffuse the conflict. The final outcome was a win-lose outcome. The service manager had most or all of his needs satisfied, while Janet had very little or none of her needs satisfied. Graphically displayed, the outcome looked something like this:

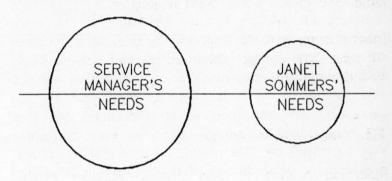

This is bound to make Janet feel defeated, and nobody likes the loser role. She will carry this feeling with her into every transaction she has with that company in the future. It probably will affect her in other transactions with other companies as well. She certainly will report her unfortunate and one-sided negotiation to her friends and to all who will listen to her tale of woe.

What does this say to us with regard to conflict resolution and dealing with people? If we take all and make the other person feel as if they have lost, we have created an enemy. We have let loose on our potential customers and clients a messenger determined to get even with us. And get even they will! In some instances it can become a veritable vendetta.

The same applies for personal and family situations. If a spouse approaches every disagreement with a win-lose attitude, the results can be disastrous. What was once an amicable relationship with understanding and love can very quickly become a raging inferno of threats, hostility and hatred.

Transfer the factors we are discussing to the work environment, and we discover the fundamental causes of misunderstanding, labour unrest and strikes. Many disputes and disagreements arise, not out of salaries and wages, but a feeling among employees on the one hand and management on the other that they are being taken advantage of. So we must find some way to dispel the frustration, hostility and anger and create more of a climate of trust. Certainly a willingness to compromise would help. Sometimes just listening will improve the climate enough for an agreement to be worked out. Sometimes just common courtesy is all that is required.

The lose-lose outcome

What would happen if we were to replace passive Janet with aggressive and belligerent Ron?

When the service manager advises Ron that his warranty has expired, Ron merely laughs at him. He then proceeds to threaten the dealership with exposure in the local paper. He talks about the letters he will write to the manufacturer and how many of his friends he will tell about the rotten deal he is receiving. The more he talks, the angrier he gets.

The service manager, an aggressive person himself, does not appreciate being told off, so he digs in his heels. He maintains the necessary work has been done, and the fault is not with the service but with the driver. They both display the stubborn side of their character and a classic impasse is arrived at. Ron demands to see the general manager and lodges a spirited complaint.

The general manager, on hearing the full story, supports his service manager, although he does not appreciate his poor negotiating skills. This is the third time over the past three months he has been brought into a service dispute. He has other things to do. He has a company to run, 55 employees to pay and sales to promote. He makes a quiet note that he needs a new service manager. This is what we call a lose-lose outcome. Lose-lose because everybody loses. The service manager, Ron, and the general manager...add to that the company, the employees and their customers.

The lose-lose graphic looks somewhat like this:

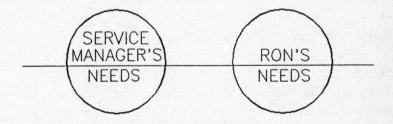

A smaller and depleted pie. Less to go around for everyone. Anger, frustration and long term animosity. Really, when you consider the losses, a pretty ridiculous and profoundly stupid outcome.

A win-win strategy

The service manager has been replaced by Tom McFarlane, seasoned veteran from the competition. Helen Black is sitting in his office complaining about her car, which she has brought in for the second time over the last three months for stalling. She talks of the frustration of having to bring back her car and the inconvenience of having to ask for time off at her place of work. Tom listens and apologizes for the inconveniences. He asks a few more probing questions and learns of the near accident Helen experienced yesterday as a result of her car stalling again. He shows genuine concern and promises to give the matter his personal attention. He advises her the warranty period has expired, but he will personally make sure that this particular problem will be looked after at no additional cost to her. Tom McFarlane has achieved a win-win outcome and the graphic illustration looks like this:

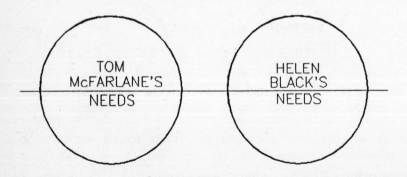

Now we have a much bigger pie! A fair agreement has been reached and both parties have gone away satisfied. A number of factors have been added to the equation. For instance, trust is a new ingredient. More than anything else, trust is a factor for ongoing positive relationships. Another ingredient is that satisfied negotiators are willing and ready to negotiate again. Their respect for each other is enhanced, and they are willing to try again. Contrast this with the win-lose outcome where the participants will avoid each other or return to the fray with a battle axe in each hand!

The win-win outcome is the target of good negotiators. Compromise, trust, respect and cooperation are hallmarks of the win-win outcome.

Chapter 2

THE CRITICAL FACTOR FOR SUCCESSFUL NEGOTIATING

Tom McFarlane is an unusual breed of manager. Instead of responding in the normal adversarial manner, he chose the route of compromise. His response is empathetic and caring. He realises there are some company needs that must be addressed, but he also realises the customer also has needs that must be satisfied. He is sharp enough to know that if these needs are not satisfied, the chances are he will never see Helen Black again.

Compromise is the middle road

Compromise is the search for a fair and satisfactory solution. It is finding the middle road. Compromise is arriving at a win-win solution through giving up a little of what we want so we can get a little of what we need. It means winning a little and losing a little in order to get our fair share of the pie.

When Jennifer Heard finally generated the courage to go into her manager's office to ask for a raise she didn't know much about compromise. Jennifer was obsessed with her low wage. There were so many things she wanted to do but couldn't. Her car was too old, and her apartment complex was noisy and sometimes the elevators didn't work. Somehow she had to make a change. The obvious answer was to get a raise, buy a new car and move to a new apartment.

When Mr. Rankin asked her why she felt she needed a raise, her reply was, "I need a new car." Mr. Rankin patiently brought to her attention that her job did not require a lot of skills. He explained that the salary she was receiving for her work was competitive with most of the other businesses in that area. "Jennifer, you are a good worker, and we really enjoy having you here. You have a sunny personality, and you really light up our office. However, there are some factors you must consider, if you hope to improve your position in the company. First, have you ever thought of taking a typing course? That would make you more valuable to us here. You could type invoices during slack periods at the reception desk. Would you consider taking a course at the company's expense?"

Jennifer thought of the time and energy, the travel and frustration of getting to and from evening school. She thought of having to miss her favourite TV programs, and her telephone calls to Eva, her best friend. But she read the message clearly from Mr. Rankin. No typing skills meant no salary increase.

Somewhere she had heard you have to give a little to get a little. Maybe this was what compromise meant. She slowly nodded her head and agreed to take the course. She heard Mr. Rankin saying that on completion of her course the company would be glad to consider raising her salary. "You see, Jennifer," he said, "there is always two sides to the equation. If you give a little more, we can give a little more too. Then both of us will feel good about the situation. It's what we call in business a win-win outcome."

Compromise means cooperation

Compromise also means cooperation. It means going contrary to the traditional, habitual, spontaneous response. We have for so long been exposed to the adversarial affliction that we unconsciously find ourselves exhibiting its symptoms. It's natural to criticize if management makes a new policy. It's a temptation to resist if our spouse comes up with a new idea. It's axiomatic to say "no" if our teenager makes a request.

An interesting experience occurred recently in a negotiation seminar I attended. The seminar leader asked participants to form into groups of two and to grasp each other's hands in the classic arm wrestling position. He then asked us to see which group of two could wrestle his or her partner's hand to the table the greatest number of times in 30 seconds.

The results were revealing. One group reported in excess of 30 times. Another group reported zero. The latter, of course, were more taken up with resisting the efforts of their partners. They saw their partners as adversaries...obstacles to achievement. The successful participants on the other hand immediately became preoccupied with cooperation and worked together to achieve the desired goal.

The saddest commentaries that come from seminar participants as they discuss their work environment is the constant use of "they."   An unknown but significant factor out there that is working against them. They are caught up in the adversarial game. They always seem to be at war. It's Union against Management, the Yankees against the Blue Jays, the Liberals against the Conservatives, or just plain little me against you.

How much more productive if we realized we are all working towards the same goal. How much easier if we changed our perspective from "you" against "me" to "you and me against the problem." Then we could combine our resources, work out some mutual goals, merge our energies and achieve fair and realistic solutions. Compromise is cooperation, and over the long haul it is more productive.

Compromise means honesty

Compromise is not compliance. It definitely is not just giving in and allowing the other side to railroad you into passive appeasement. It's being fair and strong. It means standing up for your principles and being firm in the face of threats, insensitivity and dishonesty. It means being honest, and honesty is one of the main factors for building trust and respect in business and private life. James Kouzes and Barry Posner in their recent book **The Leadership Challenge** spoke of the absolute need for honesty in a leader. They said: "In every survey we conducted, honesty was selected more than any other leadership characteristic. When you think about it, honesty is absolutely essential to leadership. After all, if we are to willingly follow someone, whether it be into battle or into the boardroom, we first want to assure ourselves that the person is worthy of our trust." Compromise is honesty and fairness and strength that eventually wins respect from the other side.

Compromise means empathy

Compromise also means exercising the fine art of empathy. Despite what you may have heard, negotiation is not just about what *YOU* want. There is another person at the end of the line. There are some wants and needs asking for attention on the other side of the equation. If we are insensitive to that need, we practically guarantee frustration and subsequently, failure.

I will never forget a participant in the very first negotiation seminar that I conducted. Harold's concern was that in nearly all of his previous negotiations he had been taken advantage of. "I always seem to come out on the losing end," he said, in a frustrated tone of voice. "Can you give me some strategies that will help me win the next time around?" In a later seminar, a participant asked for some strategies to guarantee a raise. "I have an appointment with my boss in two days to talk about a raise. I need an effective strategy." In both these scenarios, the parties seemed preoccupied with their own needs to the exclusion of the needs of the other side. As far as they were concerned, they wanted a tool that would successfully "beat the opposition" into submission. They were not prepared to listen to the needs of the other side. They lacked respect for the other side. They were short on empathy.

Defeat is sometimes victory

There are times when victory lies in being defeated. Have you ever found yourself playing a game with a friend or acquaintance, and everything was going well for you? No matter what you did, you won. You then began to sense the frustration your friend was experiencing. That was when you decided that orchestrating your own defeat might contribute more to the relationship you were trying to build. There are times when it is in our interest to give a little without getting anything. There are times when it is in our interest to give a lot without getting much in return.

A friend of mine is an expert in his field. He has the answers and is usually right. However, he has a penchant for pointing out the errors of others. He is nearly always right, but his peers tend to avoid him and in subtle ways sabotage his career. Just recently I asked him, "John, would you prefer to be right and lose our support, or wrong but have the team behind you?"

One of the hardest things I have to do is to watch people doing the wrong thing and deliberately hold my tongue, so that I give them a chance to learn through their own experience. If I intervene they would probably continue anyway...and, in nearly every instance, my criticism would have done harm to our relationship.

Of course there are times when necessity and principle dictates something should be said. You will know when that is. But so many times it wouldn't matter one way or the other. We merely want to establish our authority, or flaunt our knowledge or enhance our self-esteem at the expense of another. That might be the time to hold your tongue, or to let the statistic go unchallenged, or to just plain accept defeat.

Wise old Ben Franklin gave some good advice when he said: "If you argue and rankle and contradict, you may achieve a victory sometimes; but it will be an empty victory because you will never get your opponent's good will." There are times when compromise means accepting defeat. Giving in could result in a long-term relationship that would have greater benefits than a small short-term victory.

So don't take yourself too seriously. Don't be in too much of a hurry to challenge every little infringement of the rules. Learn to laugh at yourself.

A contemporary of mine likes to remind me consistently, "You know I always tell it the way it is!" That might sound like an admirable and commendable objective, and certainly in some instances it is. There are other times however, when it gets in the way and is nothing more than a barrier to rapport.

Compromise then is a prime factor in successful

negotiation. Approaching negotiation with a rigid attitude will probably result in a rigid attitude on the
other side, while an attitude of compromise will
quite often win concessions. It's a little like the
Australian boomerang...what you send out comes
back to you.

Chapter 3

MODIFY YOUR PERSONAL STYLE
AND GET THE RESULTS YOU WANT

Your personal style is your key to effective persuasion and win-win outcomes. It is the prime factor in achieving the kind of climate in which good things happen. It is the resource with which you can build rapport and win people to your way of thinking. If you want to influence and persuade other people, it is imperative you understand your own personal style and its impact on the people you are interacting with.

Ronald could never understand the reason why people treated him the way they did. Looking back over his career, it seemed to him that life was a minefield of problems and misfortunes. His first two jobs ended in dismissal. During his next job he was reprimanded frequently by his boss about his tendency to socialize and waste other people's time. He seemed to be always at war with some authority figure.

Ronald just could not understand what it was all about. After all he was only trying to do his job. Yes, he liked being friendly. People needed a bit of cheering up. He liked talking to people and cheering them up. What was so wrong about that? What Ronald didn't know was he tended to overdo the "cheering up" role and frustrate his fellow employees. Instead of attending to the job he was assigned to do, he invariably found someone to talk to and joke with. His loud voice travelled over the office, disturbing other employees who wanted to get their work done. They resented the interruption Ronald created, and made little remarks about it to Ronald's manager. "Why don't you get him to stay at his desk and do the work he is supposed to do?" they hinted.

Ronald's manager didn't feel too good about that. He had enough to do without monitoring Ronald and watching his every activity. His response was to give Ronald another warning. Ronald was even more confused now. He didn't understand his manager, he didn't understand his fellow employees, and he was beginning to feel he didn't understand himself.

One of the prime requirements for improving your interaction with others is to understand your own style. What kind of image are you projecting? It might come as a surprise to you to learn that you may be projecting an entirely different picture to the one you think you are projecting. Most people are not aware that they are perceived differently to the way they think they are perceived.

Here is a simple exercise that will tell you if others are seeing you the way you are seeing yourself. From the twenty words listed below, choose five words that you think best describe your personal style:

enthusiastic	mature	aggressive
indecisive	dignified	excitable
serious	weak	pushy
confident	cheerful	inconsiderate
modest	hyperactive	agreeable

calm   insensitive   sincere
unsure

Having done that, ask two or three fellow employees to choose five words from the same list that they think aptly describe your personal style. The answer should be revealing. Did they choose words you chose? Did they see you in the same way you saw yourself? Or did they choose words that had no resemblance to the ones you chose for yourself? That means they saw you in an entirely different light than you saw yourself.

Behaviourial scientists Joseph Luft and Harrington Ingram, have convincingly demonstrated that we are unaware of how we are perceived by others. Because our styles affect our ability to influence and persuade, it is important we know and understand the kind of personal style we have.

Basic behavioural styles

It is generally accepted that there are four basic behavioural styles. Let us again review and discuss them. To make this more interesting, let's ask you the reader to go along with a fun exercise that will give you some idea of the personal style you have, as well as building a base for a productive discussion about styles. On the horizontal axis shown in Figure 1, mark yourself according to the factors shown on each side of the axis. A word of warning before hastening to make your mark. Be clear in your mind what side of the mid-point of the line you are on. Reflect on the comments made about you over the years, evaluate yourself realistically, and decide if you are more of a listening person than a talking person, or vice versa? Having made that decision, decide the degree to which you are a listening person or a talking person. If you are an extremely talkative person, put your mark on the extreme right of the line. The other factors may help you to begin to see yourself in a more objective way. At best though, it will be a subjective exercise, and as this is not promoted as a scientifically-correct conclusion, it will not matter much.

Now let's turn our attention to the vertical axis. Again, evaluate the comments of others over the years. Consider your own assessment of your self and decide whether you are a warm, emotional person or a disciplined, businesslike person. Your immediate reaction may be that you are both at different times. You are probably correct, but you may also agree that you are more comfortable with one of those styles. You consistently react to situations with behaviour more oriented towards "fun loving and impulsive" or "serious and businesslike.". Don't consider this to be a test. Have fun with it.

You now have a mark on the horizontal axis and a mark on the vertical axis. Draw a horizontal and vertical line from each of these marks in such a way that they intersect at a certain point. Put a large X at the intersection of these lines as shown in Figure. 2. You have just identified your personal style!

Now draw a line completely around the two axis lines so that you form a large square (see Figure 2).

FIGURE 1
BEHAVIOURAL STYLES

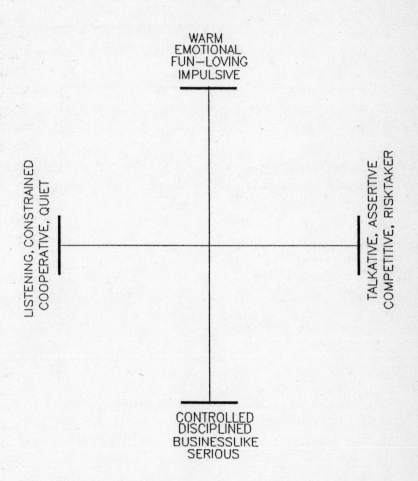

We now have four quadrants, which represent the four basic behavioural styles. You, of course, are in one of those quadrants and will be interested in knowing the characteristics of your own style, as well as the characteristics of the other three styles

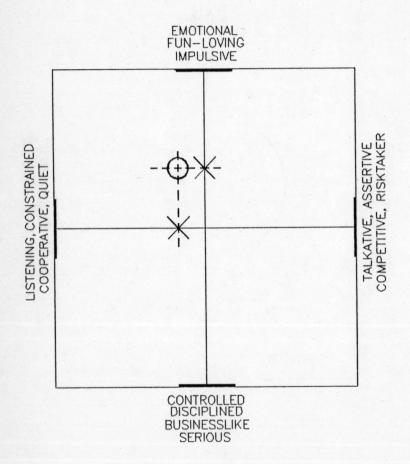

FIGURE 2
YOUR STYLE

EMOTIONAL
FUN—LOVING
IMPULSIVE

LISTENING, CONSTRAINED
COOPERATIVE, QUIET

TALKATIVE, ASSERTIVE
COMPETITIVE, RISKTAKER

CONTROLLED
DISCIPLINED
BUSINESSLIKE
SERIOUS

First, let's name the quadrants and then we will
proceed to describe the behaviour associated with
each quadrant. Figure 3 shows the quadrants complete with names as follows: FRIENDLY,
DOMINANT, EXPRESSIVE, CAUTIOUS.

FIGURE 3
FOUR BASIC STYLES

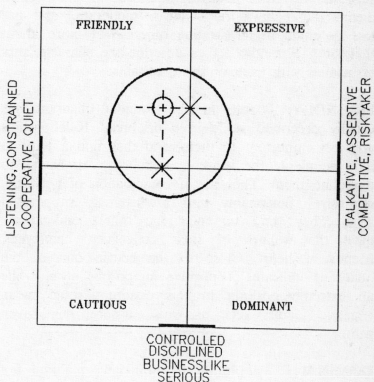

These are the four basic behavioural styles, and
each of us can be placed in one of these quadrants.
This does not mean we are fully and completely in
that quadrant to the exclusion of the others. What
it really means is we have an orientation towards

that behavioural style. We are partial towards that way of expressing ourselves. We are more comfortable as we exhibit the behaviour represented by that quadrant.

The way we are positioned in the quadrant is quite significant also. Extreme distance from the centre suggests extreme behaviour. Close to the centre means our behavioural style is "moderate," and has less potential for frustrating others. But more about that later. For now, let us describe the characteristics associated with each of the quadrants.

FRIENDLY: People in the friendly quadrant are usually described as "people oriented." Relationships are very important to them, and they find it hard to hurt people in the sense of saying "no" or having to discipline them. They are a combination of a "warm, impulsive" personality and a "listening, supportive" style. They tend to encourage others and always have the welfare of their colleagues, employees, friends at heart. Close to the centre-point of the quadrant indicates a positive supportive style, while an extreme position in this quadrant could mean negative factors such as weak, unsure, mild, even wimpy.

DOMINANT: People in the dominant quadrant are "task oriented." They are preoccupied with getting things done. They are the movers and shakers. They are always concerned about delivery. Because of their preoccupation with results, they sometimes overlook the feelings and emotions of people. They might even look at people as instruments to help them in their efforts to obtain results. In some instances, they might forget that people are human beings like themselves. The result of all this is that people in this quadrant are sometimes seen as insensitive, inconsiderate, pushy and harsh. Their overbearing style tends to turn people off. They get things done, but sometimes at the expense of losing friends, employees and relatives.

CAUTIOUS: The person in this quadrant is a combination of "serious" and "listener." This person is the observing type. They are cautious in their approach to decisions and tend to want as much information as is possible to get. While this is a desirable characteristic, they tend to take it beyond a realistic point; and it results in frustration for others. They often bottle-neck the flow of information or work schedules, because they need more information for an incidental decision. They tend to be suspicious, indecisive and partial towards delaying things. While this factor is valuable when an appropriate amount of it is shown, it can get to be quite frustrating when a person becomes overly cautious.

EXPRESSIVE: The expressive person is a sales person. Not necessarily with regard to his or her career, but certainly as it relates to style. They are a combination of "warm" and "talkative" and find it easy to express themselves in positive ways. They make friends easily, but sometimes, depending on how extreme they are in this quadrant, tend to tire people with their excessive talk and high spirits. When they are well placed in their quadrant, they can be very influential and certainly make great sales people. An extreme position in the quadrant suggests a person who may be hyperactive and excitable, and in some instances may be manipulative.

So there you have it! The four basic personality styles. You may have found a little of yourself in each of the descriptions. That is the way it should be. We all have some of each of the styles, but we each also have a larger proportion of one of the styles.

Ingredients of style

Where does style come from? How did that unique assortment of attitudes, values, prejudices, emotions and fears develop? Never before and never again will all the elements that make up that composite you ever come together again in exactly the same way they have come together in you. You are a miracle, and you need to remind yourself of that everyday. But how did all this happen?

There are a number of different perspectives on this. For instance, two of the founding fathers of modern psychology and psychiatry maintained that personality is formed in the first few years of life. Sigmund Freud taught that "the essential foundations of character are laid down by the age of three and ... later events can modify but not alter the traits established." Alfred Adler, who disagreed with Freud on so many things, dates the adaptation of a permanent life-style at age four or five.

Maxwell Maltz, popular author of **Psychocybernetics,** maintains that human personality is moulded in the first five years of our lives. Many respected psychologists today agree. They maintain that the brain is like an unprogrammed computer and data input in the early years forms a foundation that eventually develops into a personality style. This style will seldom change throughout a person's lifetime. It might be modified, but the basic style of personality, - assertive, passive or cautious - will tend to remain much the same all through a person's life.

Another view of the origin of the style that you have is that it was formed before you ever came into the world.   You were influenced in your mother's womb, and your personality formed there. Thomas Verny, M.D. writes in his book, **The Secret Life of the Unborn Child,** that the fetus is capable of hearing before birth. He suggests the unborn child hears and responds to the life taking place on the outside of its temporary home. At birth, the child has already been exposed to certain influences and already has a personality and a style. Carl Jung, one of the fathers of modern psychology, assumed that some basic tendencies of a person's psychological type are part of his genetic inheritance.

To support this theory, those of us who reared children found it remarkable that our children showed certain tendencies within the first three to four months after birth and were amazed that these tendencies grew stronger with time.

For instance, I have a contemporary whose eldest daughter is expressive and articulate. These characteristics appeared in the early months after birth. She didn't speak, but she did the closest thing to it. His other daughter is quiet and unassuming. She never spoke until she was three years old. In other words the early indicators of their personalities, evident during the first two to three months after birth, were confirmed as the years went by. Perhaps we are indeed born with our personalities.

Another perspective on our personal style is that we brought it with us from another life. Proponents of reincarnation are confident we lived before. They maintain that in another life we developed a personality, which we brought with us to this life. This personality is the result of lessons learned through various experiences and explains why some people seem so advanced and able to cope; while others never seem to be able to handle the challenges of life. When this perspective is ridiculed, reincarnationists usually point to child prodigies like Mozart and Beethoven and their ability to accomplish tasks a normal person can do only after years of intense study and practice. The enigma of child prodigies seem to have no other explanation than they were exposed to previous experiences.

In any event, we find ourselves with a personality or style that stays with us throughout our lifetime. Robert and Dorothy Bolton in their excellent book, **Social Style/Management Style,** declare that after intense investigation they have not been able to establish one authentic example of a change in personality style. Perhaps a maturing or a modifying, but not a change. So, you are stuck with what you have!

However, what you have is right for you. There are no fundamentally bad or good styles. Successful people are found in the four basic styles. Within these four fundamental styles, there are both positive and negative personality traits. But the essential style you exhibit is neither successful nor unsuccessful. It's just you!

Regardless of how you came to have your present style, it is a composite of attitudes, values, prejudices and fears. Life's experiences have strengthened and reinforced your beliefs, and the composite you is expressed through language and non-verbal communication. These form a behavioural pattern that is perceived as uniquely you. You will be known as a "reliable person who is easy to get along with," or you may be known as a "rather difficult person who is quite often abrasive." You might also be the kind of person people describe as an "outspoken but sensitive person, and we know where we are with you."

Some people are known "as rather withdrawn and difficult to read." These statements are general statements that describe how others see you most of the time. All of us will have times when we depart from the image we habitually project. But there is always a distinct set of behaviours we become associated with and our peers, relatives and friends come to identify as us. This is our style.

The impact of style

Your style is what people see. It is the behavioural
robe you wear, and others assess you by it. People
you interact with take away a certain impression you
make on them. They remember you because of
certain things you do and the way in which you do
them. Your dress may have a certain character to it.
You may greet them with a smile and a firm handshake, which signals confidence. To reinforce this you
may have positive eye contact, which further serves
to emphasize a high-confidence level. Your whole
demeanor presents an atmosphere of confidence and
friendliness, and the other person receives a very
positive impression of you. Contrast this with
someone whose style gives a negative message. This
person finds it hard to make positive eye contact
and dresses inappropriately. Facial expressions convey
a message of frustration and despair. Your enthusiasm towards dealing with this person is going to be
much less than with the more positive person previously described.

People carry away an impression that you make on
them through your particular style, regardless of the
actual words you use. I can personally picture people
I met two decades ago and remember the kind of
style they exhibited. For instance, my old college
principal was a dignified, white-haired, humorous dis-
ciplinarian. After forty-five years I can still recall the
respect we young boys had for him. I can't remember any specific words he said, but I certainly can

remember how our behaviour changed when he was in sight. The cry of "Old D" was enough to discourage the most daring trouble maker in our group. Mr. Davis made an indelible impression on my mind, and I am sure on the minds of hundreds of other school contemporaries.

People will often forget our names, may even forget our faces, but very seldom our styles. What we are as a person: kind, loving, caring and friendly or hard, insensitive and selfish stands out and is remembered long after our words are forgotten. So our personal style is perhaps more of a label than even our name. People will forget our name but very seldom the kind of person we are. Our style makes a lasting impact on others.

Power and style

Your style has a powerful influence on other people. Whatever you do in an interaction will prompt some response from the other person. People are always reacting to what we say, what we do, and how we do it. Style then is a medium by which we get reactions, and these reactions can be both favourable or unfavourable.

Just as in the world of physics, there is a law that says for every cause there is an effect, so in the world of interpersonal activities every action has a reaction. It behoves us then to examine the kind of reactions we get from others. For instance, what kind of reaction do we get if we actively listen to another person? What kind of reaction do we get if

we talk incessantly? What kind of reaction do we get
if we act in a friendly manner? When viewed from
this perspective, style becomes a powerful instrument.
Theoretically, all we need to know is the kinds of
actions that result in favourable reactions, and we
have opened a magic box of goodies! For instance,
could we find certain actions that would result in
people immediately liking us? Could we find a particular kind of behaviour that would result in a job
promotion?

I find it such a pleasure to be with Beulah. She has
a sensitive style that allows her to do her fair share
of listening. When she makes a point she usually
says it in a way that does not convey finality. There
is always room for error or for change if there is
more information. Our conversation becomes a pleasant exchange of ideas. A discussion with her is
always a joy and a pleasure. I want to do things for
Beulah. Her considerate and interested style has won
me over, and she only needs to ask and I will
respond positively to any reasonable request.

On the other hand, I can think of a number of
people I try to avoid, rather than try to have a
meaningful discussion with them. They present their
ideas with little room for discussion or comment.
They leave me feeling obligated to accept their point
of view or start an argument or a war. Rather than
an exchange of ideas, our discussion becomes a one-
sided display of arrogance and insensitivity. My
opinions are never even considered.

Is it any wonder that in the company of such people
we avoid any invitation for discourse? The only good

thing that comes out of such an encounter is a lesson in how to build tension and frustration. In other words, it rings warning bells in my mind and helps to make me more sensitive to the feelings of others. It dramatically illustrates that when you talk with someone you are either building tension or you are building rapport. Your actions, your tone of voice and the words you use either build a wall of disagreement leading to impasse or a positive, receptive environment resulting in a win-win outcome.

Style modification

Psychologists maintain that our basic personality style cannot be changed, but it is possible to modify our style. As a matter of fact, that is something we do on a daily basis. For instance, are you the same person at home that you are at work? Or do you find yourself modifying your style just a little in order to cope with the different scenarios that exist at work.

I worked for a man who was an absolute tyrant during working hours. This meant a conscious modifying of my style to cope with my work situation. There was an interesting twist to this story however. As soon as the work day was done, he became a friendly and considerate person. He was actually a lot of fun after working hours. Every morning he consciously modified his style to fit the occasion as he saw it. He was a master at modifying his style.

Some of us have to modify our style out of

necessity. If your boss is a strong, demanding, auto-
cratic person, and you happen to have some of the
same personality characteristics, you might find exhibiting the same personality style is too stressful and
frustrating. Short of leaving your job, you might have
no alternative but to modify your style and exhibit a
more passive role. We are not proposing a Dr Jeykl
and Mr. Hyde replay here, but rather a small
modification in your behaviour patterns - just enough
to soften or perhaps intensify your style to ease
tension. In a later chapter we will show how style
can help to build rapport as you modify and more
closely resemble the style of the other person.

The power of flexibility

It is natural to think that modifying your style to
accomplish certain objectives could be interpreted as
manipulation. Certainly if the intent is to misinform,
mislead or deceive in any way, there would be
reason for concern. But style modification is merely
a tool we are already using on a constant basis,
even if unconsciously. The intent here is to create
awareness of a tool that can help to lessen stress,
break through to people and communicate more
effectively.

Flexibility, which is nothing more than style modification, is one of the prime requirements, if not the
prime requirement for good interpersonal skills. Over
and over in surveys, managers and CEOs, who surface as effective communicators, are the ones able
to adjust to different kinds of personalities and meet
them at their level. These leaders are flexible, sensit-

ive to the varying personalities of others and able to adjust at a moment's notice to the differences they sense in the other person.

It is people that cannot adjust who fail and cause tension and distress to develop among others. They fail to sense the differences, continuing to maintain their own agendas, and upset and frustrate the other person.

This quality of flexibility is invaluable, and a high price is paid for it. It means understanding other people and the agendas they come with, adjusting to their style through style modification, and monitoring the ongoing interplay of action and reaction. Flexibility results in satisfactory agreements and win-win outcomes.

Perhaps the most dramatic illustration of flexibility in my experience was watching Bill at work. Bill was the national sales manager with a construction equipment leasing company I worked with years ago. Bill was just as much at home on a large construction site as he was in the president's office. He knew just how to relax and be one of the boys as he talked with an equipment operator, and then adjust at a moment's notice to a more formal and professional behaviour as he met with the president in his prestigious office. He didn't change as a person, as the same respect was afforded both, but some subtle changes in adjusting to the interests of each person was evident. He was able to be like the operator in his environment, and like the president in his environment. Bill was a very persuasive person. He understood the power of flexibility.

Chapter 4

19 STRATEGIES THAT BUILD RAPPORT, CREATE A POSITIVE IMPACT AND REDUCE TENSION

You are a message

"The way you are perceived affects the way you are treated," says Buck Rogers of IBM fame. What message do you project? How do people treat you? These two questions are inextricably linked and are at the core of building rapport, improving interpersonal relationships and persuading others.

My friend Tom told me an interesting story over coffee. He said he was standing in line at one of the quick copy outlets some weeks ago. Before him was a man with a large quantity of original project sheets, evidently for copying. It was about 4:00 p.m. on a Friday afternoon. Tom said he couldn't help feeling that he would be standing in line for a long time, if this man wanted all of his printing done immediately.

Tom had a significant amount of printing to be done also. He had procrastinated on getting to the printer, and now he had to get this done as he needed it for a Saturday seminar. He told me he listened carefully as the man addressed the attendant behind the counter. Throwing down the mound of project sheets, the man casually advised the attendant that he needed 50 copies of each of the project sheets immediately. The attendant responded by advising him that as it was close to closing time he could have the printing some time on Monday. In a rather condescending voice the man then proceeded to tell the attendant that he had invested hundreds of dollars in a seminar that was taking place tomorrow. He had to have the copies immediately. The attendant was visibly upset at the man's aggressive attitude and condescending manner. He again repeated that the printing could not be done until Monday.

The man then exploded into a series of expletives and demanded to speak with the manager. The attendant immediately went to the phone, got his manager, whispered a few words to him, and then handed the aggressive customer the phone. It was impossible to hear the other side of the conversation, but the final outcome was that the aggressive, condescending customer walked through the door with his mound of project sheets not copied.

The sequel to this was that the person immediately before Tom had a significant amount of printing to be done also. As a matter of fact, the total of her printing and his amounted to about the same that the belligerent customer had. Yet their printing got done, and Mr. Belligerent left with his undone.

■ *Ask for help*

When the lady before Tom spoke to the clerk, she said: "I hope you can help me. I am sorry I have so much printing at this time on a Friday afternoon when we are all thinking of going home and having a nice weekend. But I just had so much to do today that I am only now getting here. Do you think you could manage to run these for me now?" The answer: "Well, let me see what I can do." When Tom got to the counter his first words were, "I need your help too. Do you think you could manage this for me?"

The clerk responded to the total message that was communicated, rather than just the words. He saw the first person as a belligerent, abrasive, condescending person. A man who had no respect for the person doing the job of running a printing machine. His whole demeanor and image shouted a message to the clerk: "You are here to serve me! I am a customer, and the customer is always right. I must have this printing immediately. How dare you suggest that I can't have this until Monday?" The result was a defense response on the part of the attendant: "So you think you can push me around. Well, I have some power too. I'm going to make sure that you don't get your printing done today. Just watch me!"

Was the request that different from the lady's and Tom's? Not really. They were all asking the attendant to do their printing, late on a Friday afternoon.

But the image each projected was quite different. The lady was asking the clerk to help her. She acknowledged that she was at fault in leaving the printing so late. Could he help her. She was sincere in this respect. It was evident in her voice intonation, in her facial expression, in her voice volume and in her gestures. The clerk's response? "I want to help this lady. She needs my assistance and I think I can help her." The response to Tom's request was much the same. They both got their printing done.

Asking for help is one of the most powerful ways to build rapport. To me, some of the most persuasive words in the English language are, "I wonder if you can help me?" I have found out that people really want to help you. Yes, they do! If you ask them in the right way, people will bend over backwards to help. Sometimes I am actually embarassed at the length people will go to when I ask for help. I can't count the number of times I have asked for help in a hotel, and some member of the staff has left what he was doing to personally lead me to a room or deliver some kind of service. Of course, we might say that that's his or her job. Sure, but look at the number of times people don't get that kind of service.

What kind of image do you project as you go about your daily activities? How do people think of you and perceive you? Are you a good listener and easy to be with? On the other hand are you confrontational and abrasive, always ready for a fight? Do you often create some kind of unpleasant scene? Whatever it might be, you do leave an impression with others. You are thought of and remembered in a certain way. You can't avoid it. Your total message is being communicated everyday, and you leave that message in the minds of everyone you meet. This can be critical in your career and your relationships, as well as in your ability to influence and persuade others.

■ *Don't depend on words only*

Some years ago I owned and operated an employment agency. In discussions with my colleagues and from my own experience, I discovered that it only took three to four minutes to decide if an applicant was suited for a certain job or not. Within that short time they told me so much about themselves, I was able to decide whether I was going to send them on a certain job interview or not. I very seldom changed after continuing the interview. In many instances it was just a courtesy to continue, as I had already made up my mind in the first two minutes.

Studies have been made about the image we project with some rather interesting and startling answers. None more startling than Albert Meharabian's statistic that breaks down the message that you are into three mediums: the words we speak, the voice intonations as we deliver those words, and the body language we use to support the message. Meharabian then went on to identify the mediums in the order of their importance. Here they are: He said body language is by far the most important, and he gave that 55 per cent of the equation. Next was the voice intonations and tone that we use as we communicate. He gave that 38 per cent. The words which actually carry the content of the message he gave only 7 per cent. According to Meharabian and indeed many other experts such as Roger Ailes (communication consultant to President Reagan and President Bush and author of **You are the Message**), the words we speak carry only a small part of the message we are trying to communicate. In the minds of those we communicate with, voice intonations and body language are far more meaningful. Very shortly we will look at the elements of body language that signal such a powerful message, but in the meantime, a good question to ask yourself would be, "What message am I projecting?" Make no mistake about it, *YOU* are a message!

The structure of image

What is it that makes potential employers make up their minds about you in two to three minutes? What are you saying to them that is so significant? Indeed you hardly have time to shake hands and sit down and make some small talk about the weather, before two minutes have gone by. And it is exactly in those activities that you are giving a message that can adversely affect you. On the other hand, you might in those first two minutes communicate a message that immediately gets your potential employer on your side, to look for things to confirm she wants to employ you.

As an employment counsellor, I met a young couple that made quite an impression on my mind. The husband, who we will call Dave, projected a poor image and subsequently was not able to influence or persuade potential employers to employ him. His wife on the other hand, had such a pleasant personality that she nearly always ended up with three or four job offers in the space of a week or two. I had the opportunity of working with this young couple over a period of two years. My introduction to them was immediately after they had graduated from university and gotten married. They both were very intelligent young people and successful in their university careers. Dave graduated as an engineer and Judy as a psychologist. Despite Dave's credentials, he had a problem getting a job. As a matter of fact despite a significant number of interviews that I sent him on, he was not able to get a job offer for six months. He became quite discouraged.

Judy's story was quite different, however. One week after I met her, I sent her on five job interviews and she received three job offers. Because of Dave's inability to secure a position they decided Toronto was perhaps not the place for them. Through some connections Dave was able to get a responsible position in Northern Ontario. Two years later they returned to Toronto. By this time Dave had gained in confidence and his image was a lot stronger. After a month or two we were able to get him into a responsible position in which he stayed for many years. Again, Judy was a different story. Within two weeks of her return to Toronto she ended up with four job offers. What was it that these two young people communicated that allowed one to have dramatic success, while the other experienced discouraging failure? They both had the same credentials. They both were young and healthy, and they both were intelligent. Could the answer have been, a positive and attractive image? Image is made up of many parts. The ingredients of the composite YOU are varied. Some elements that immediately and dramatically affect the way you are perceived are dress, facial expression, posture, eye contact, touch and voice.

■ *Dress for success*

How you are perceived affects the way you are treated. If your appearance signals to others that you are careless about dressing appropriately, they draw conclusions from that. Only last night I was talking to a colleague of mine who complained bitterly about how a speaker dressed for a presentation we attended. My friend pointed out that the members of the audience were far more suitably dressed than the speaker himself. He criticized the speaker for not wearing a tie or jacket, while the majority of the audience wore jackets and ties. He found fault with the content of the speaker's presentation and the style he used to present.

Indeed, the dress of the speaker was just as my colleague described. But I noticed something even more significant. My colleague was inclined to be more critical of the speaker because he had formed his initial impression of the speaker as a careless person. I also noticed the inappropriate dress, but I tried to focus on the message of the speaker. I found some good and helpful content. My point is that inappropriate dress can bias people's minds to the point that they will not hear what you are saying. A wise old philosopher once said, "What you are shouts so loudly that I cannot hear what you are saying."

■ *Smile and change the climate*

It has been said that it takes a lot more facial muscles to frown than to smile. A smile says so much. "I like you." "What can I do for you?" "I am happy with myself." It changes the climate and the chemistry between two people. As a speaker, it says to an audience, "I am glad to be here and I'm enjoying myself." As an influencer and a persuader, it creates a climate for cooperation.

When I arrived at a seminar I was conducting a few days ago, one of the participants was already there. I greeted her with what I thought was a pleasant voice and a smile. Her response was something that sounded like a grunt or a growl, and her facial expression rather matched her sour mood. The image she communicated said to me in no uncertain terms, "Please leave me alone. I am not your friendly type, and I am not here to socialize. If you are the seminar leader, just do your job and educate me. That's what I am here for." That's the way she remained throughout the day. The rest of the participants responded much more positively. As a result, I tended to ask them a lot more questions and discuss more issues with them. As a matter of fact, I gave up my whole lunch period to discuss an issue with someone who had responded much more positively than Miss Grouch. Would I have taken the time to discuss an issue with Miss Grouch, if she had asked me? Absolutely yes! But she seemed to create a wall between us by her attitude expressed through negative facial expression, and my response was to accept that message and keep my distance.

■ *Hold your head high*

Can you pick out people that have served in the army? Can you tell if a stranger has a low self image and confidence level? My mind immediately goes to a young lady of good family background and social status. Yet, this young lady projects an image of uncertainty, indecisiveness and failure. She does it through her poor posture. As she walks into a room, her body is bent over and her eyes are on the ground. She walks with quick, hurried steps to the nearest chair or to a corner of the room. As she sits down her head is bent over and her eyes continue looking at the ground. She is a picture of dejection and fear.

I know another young lady who is quite the opposite. She enters a room with a loud voice, head high, challenging eye contact and invasion of other people's personal space. Her posture shouts at you, "I am here! I want immediate attention from you. Acknowledge me and listen to me. If you don't, I'm going to continue this aggressive approach until you do."

Somewhere between these two extremes we need to find a place. A positive image is not created by retreating into the dark recesses of a room. Neither is it by focussing the sunlight of your personality

with such intensity that everyone must give you their
absolute attention. People do not want to be com-
manded to listen to you or to notice you. A more
persuasive way is to win their attention and draw
them to you.

Pearl Graham is a good example of this kind of
personality and image. When she walks into a room
her head is high, her eye contact is suitably positive
and she wears a radiant smile. She doesn't say
much, except for a gentle "Hi" or an acknowledgement with a slight nod of the head and that radiant
smile. Her voice is quiet and controlled, and her
whole demeanor says, "I am here, but don't do
anything differently from what you were doing before
I came in. Don't worry about me, I'll find a group
after a while and make myself at home. It's nice to
be here and I am going to enjoy myself. Gee, you
all look so good."

When we were little children my mother did something for us which I did not quite understand at the
time. She made my sisters and me put a book on
our heads and walk around the room. It was fun for
us, but even more important, it helped us hold our
heads high, our shoulders back and our posture
positive. In effect, it helped us to say with our
posture, "I feel good about myself. I am comfortable
with who I am and I don't need to do unusual
things to get attention."

■ *Speak with your eyes*

We have all heard the cliche, "The eyes are the mirror of the soul." It's more than a cliche though. It's absolutely true. There is no part of our physical personality that says so much as the eyes. The eyes can cut and hurt, they can instruct, they can communicate sorrow, and they can caress and love. The eyes are powerful mediums of communication.

You probably use an elevator a lot. Have you ever noticed the different ways people in an elevator use their eyes? Some will avoid your eyes when you enter the elevator. They will not acknowledge you in any way. Their body language will tell you that you did not enter the elevator, and as far as they are concerned you really do not exist. On the other hand, others will acknowledge you with a moment of eye contact, a nod or a smile. Some might even go so far as to say "Hi." But it all started with the eyes.

Have you ever gone to a lecture, seminar or business presentation and found that the speaker had a habit of looking at his notes rather than at the audience? Did you find the presentation interesting? What did you think of the speaker? Most people find a speaker who is more interested in his notes than making eye contact with the audience quite uninteresting.

Poor eye contact will send a very negative message

to your colleagues and friends. In some instances that might be quite contrary to the truth. I know a young man who is an intelligent, academically successful and ambitious person. However, he consistently avoids eye contact with colleagues and friends. As a result some think of him as a shy, incompetent and indecisive kind of person. I would be afraid to recommend him for a job, although his academic achievements are commendable. All this might sound unfair, and it probably is. The fact is that is the way it is. People are forming impressions of you as you go about your daily activities. The way you hold yourself, the eye contact you make, the facial expressions you exhibit. All these leave an indelible message with those you come in contact with. They respond to that total image and treat you accordingly. Remember Buck Rogers' message: "The way you are perceived affects the way you are treated."

■ *Warm-up your handshake*

This is always a fun time in seminars. We have a lot of laughs when we talk about handshakes. There are so many kinds. There are the people that give you three fingers; then there are those who give you their whole hand, but with no life or pressure; there are those who enter into a "hand crushing" contest and leave you in pain; and then there are the movers and shakers who literally lift you off the ground with their enthusiasm. Finally, there are those who won't let go, and you are left in a quandary: "how can I extricate myself from this embrace?"

I don't know that I would go so far as to say that

handshaking is an art. However, it does require some attention. Some years ago I met with a group of successful consultants for a networking meeting. At one point the discussion meandered into the area of handshaking, and we ended up practising handshakes.

An important point in shaking hands is to give the person your whole hand. Make sure the "web" (that portion of the hand between the thumb and fore finger) meets with your partner's web. That done, close the fingers around your partner's fingers. Now comes the crucial point: make sure that a gentle pressure is applied, equal to the pressure being applied by your partner. The ideal is that the pressure being applied by both parties is comfortable and pleasant.

For a well-known and well-liked colleague, it is acceptable for the other hand to be placed over her hand giving a sort of double handshake. What this says is, "I like you. You are very special, and I am glad to be with you." The "double handshake" is not recommended for acquaintances or initial meetings with strangers. It makes the other party uncomfortable, and the inward response might be, "Why are you so friendly? I hardly know you. What do you want from me?" Be careful also to complete the handshake appropriately. Holding the hand too long can give a bad impression. As soon as pressure has been applied for one or two seconds, the job has been done and you should let go.

■ *Add vitality to your voice*

The moment you open your mouth people form an impression. "He must be a manager. What a beautiful resonant voice he has. I can tell he has a position of authority." Or it might be, "Her voice tells me she is a confident person, and I believe she can help us with the problem we are addressing." No matter how unattractive and uninteresting your voice is, you can improve it. We are not talking about changing the pitch or level of your voice, but rather some elements that will help to add more vitality and animation. People are turned off by a monotone voice. What it says is that the owner is a boring, dull and lifeless individual who will not add anything to our experience. Those with vital, attractive and enthusiastic voices are saying: "I have a love for life. I am enjoying the experience, and I can add to your experience also."

If you listen to a radio announcer you will notice a certain quality and cadence to his voice. Actually you will notice four distinct elements: pitch, pace, power and passion. An attractive voice will vary itself in these four areas.

Pitch is the upper and lower limits of your voice. Although we all have significant range in the pitch of our voices, many people tend to speak in a monotone voice. They consistently use one level or pitch of voice and consequently lose a sense of vitality and life. Listen to interesting and vital people and you will find a lot of their enthusiasm is expressed through their variation in pitch.

Then pace. Pace is the speed and rhythm that you speak with. Some people speak at a fast pace and never pause. This will confuse the most intelligent and alert person. Speaking without pauses is unforgivable. Pauses allow your listeners to digest, assimilate and understand what you are saying. With appropriate pauses it is almost impossible to speak too fast. Most of the top speakers in North America speak at a tremendous pace. Nevertheless they are completely understandable, because of the pauses they inject into their speech. Fast speech, with appropriate pauses, also makes you more exciting as a speaker whether it be to an audience or in a one-on-one encounter.

Lack of power in your speaking style suggests you are unsure of what you are talking about, or would prefer if it was not heard. It definitely is a signal of your confidence level. A shy, uncertain and indecisive person will nearly always have a voice that can hardly be heard. They are always being asked, "What did you say?" or "Please speak up." To make your voice more attractive, improve your pitch, pace and power variation. How do you do that? Simple! Read out loud. Take a book, poem or newspaper, lock yourself in a room if you are self-conscious, and read out loud. However, there is a special way you need to read. You are going to exaggerate or overly dramatize the material you are reading. A good illustration of how to read for improved vitality and spice is to read as if you are reading to a five-year-old. You know what you would do then, don't you? You would put life, excitement and fun into your reading. You would become a great story-teller, with all the nuances of voice to convey the roar of a lion or the plaintive cry of a little lamb. As you perform this childish exercise, you may not realize it but you will be gradually adopting a much more interesting and dynamic style of speaking. The result will be a more interesting voice.

Another element of voice is passion. Some people have no passion. Or at least they never express it in the sense of communicating what they care about. They might express anger, jealousy or fear, but that's another matter. What we are talking about now are the more positive elements of passion such as love, empathy, caring and appreciation. When last did you thank someone for something they did and really make it sound as if you meant it? People can tell when you mean something by what they hear in your voice.

■ *Bridge the gap with sincerity*

We can smile like Ginger Rogers, speak like Clark Gable, dress like Princess Diana, but if we haven't got the quality of sincerity we will be found out for what we are - a fake! All the qualities we have talked about can be enhanced and improved, but without an inward quality to support them, they will be counterproductive. The inner *you* must be genuine and sincere. In the final analysis, **Sincerity** is the most important factor in creating the right image. If you have sincerity, your words might come out wrong, your posture might not be right, your handshake might lack, but there still will be a quality about you that will bridge the gap between you and your partner and you will reach her: It might be in your eyes that she will read the message, or in the timbre and cadence of your voice, or the way you gesture to say the things you want to say.

Getting things right inside is of course another book. It deals with the kinds of pictures you consistently retain in your mind. The thoughts you think. If you think about anger, jealousy and the faults of others, you will develop the kind of image that says to people you are judging them and finding them wanting. If you encourage thoughts of patience, tolerance and love, you will say to people with your composite *you,* "I accept you for what you are. I know you can grow and improve, as indeed I can too. I will be patient with you, as I hope you will be with me. Let us share with each other and together build a better *you* and *me."*

■ *Make your message congruent*

Next time you watch a television program and the picture becomes distorted, be aware of a very important factor. Although the words are coming through clearly and audibly, the distorted picture begins to upset and confuse you to the point that you will probably not hear the message. The static in one of the mediums of communication is confusing the entire message and the impact is lost. The message lacks congruency, and the audience loses the meaning. When you communicate you actually use three mediums to deliver your message: words, voice intonation and body language. If there is static in the message, if one of the mediums is distorted, if there is lack of congruency, then the message will not have the impact it should have.

This is never more evident than when a speaker is addressing an audience. If the speaker declares he is delighted to be with that particular audience, but gives them poor eye contact, inaudible voice volume and uncertain voice intonations, the audience sees discrepancies. Their silent response will probably be a cynical "Sure!" This speaker is off to a bad start. He has hardly introduced himself and already his audience is mistrusting him. Unless he makes a dramatic change in his style, his audience will probably lose interest in a minute or two, and very shortly he will be talking to himself. His audience will have mentally deserted him and become more concerned with what is next on the program, or what they will have for supper that evening.

Congruency is a prime ingredient for establishing sincerity. When all communication mediums are aligned and in harmony, the audience interprets the communication as sincere. Greet a colleague with a smile and a warm handshake, positive eye contact and the appropriate voice intonation, and your colleague will detect sincerity and respond in like manner.

■ *Give respect and empathy*

If you could find a way to instantly impact people
positively, would you use it? If you could get people
on your side and get them working for you, would
you do it? If you could break through the barriers
of suspicion, apprehension and fear and win
people's trust, would you do it? A small incident
will illustrate my point. A few weeks ago I took the
train to Ottawa. I promised my wife I would call
her from the station and tell her where my car was
parked so she could pick it up. However, when I
got to the station with only ten minutes to spare, I
found I did not have change to make the phone
call. The station is quite isolated with no con-
venience stores, or indeed any facility for purchasing
snacks. I was in a quandary. How would I get the
change to make the phone call? Looking across at
the registration booth I saw a sign stating clearly:
NO CHANGE. No doubt many travellers had been
in the same situation I now found myself in, and
the clerk in the booth had been forced to implement a policy of "no change."

Nevertheless I approached the gentleman sitting
behind the glass and with a rather uncertain smile I
said, "I wonder if you can help me. I have a real
problem. I promised to call my wife before I take
the train, and I find I have no change. Do you
think you could change a dollar?" "Oh sure," he
said, and promptly dug into his till to supply the
required four quarters. While he was in the process

of making the change, I said to him matter of factly,
"I guess you get a lot of people asking for change."
I'll never forget his reply. It taught me a profound
lesson. A lesson that we would do well to learn and
act on. "Oh yes," he said, "I do get a lot of people
asking for change, and depending on how they ask
me, I say "yes" or "no." He looked up and gave me
a knowing smile. It was his way of saying, "Thank
you for asking with respect and empathy."

Rapport is the ability to break down barriers, build
trust and get people to want to help you. Have you
ever taken your dog for a walk and watched what
happens when your dog meets a strange dog? The
hair on the back of their necks rise, they growl, they
look suspiciously at each other and they carefully
take each other's measure as they slowly circle one
another. Then, as no evidence of attack surfaces they
become courageous and approach each other. They
smell each other and make little noises suggesting
friendship. In a short time, they are cavorting about
as if they were old friends. They have built rapport.

The same thing happens with humans. When we
meet someone for the first time we usually are
suspicious and wary. We don't "know" this person.
We have no idea what their motives and hidden
agendas might be. We are on the lookout for signs
that will reveal whether we should fight or run away.
As soon as we get the right signals, we are ready to
"play." If it is a business transaction, we become
reasonable. We listen and acknowledge what the
other person is saying. We are ready to compromise
so that a win-win outcome can be achieved.

But if the signals are wrong, we immediately resort to our defense strategy. We will not give out any information that could be used against us. We play our cards close to our chest, and even look for loopholes where we can gain an advantage. In short, we are on the attack. Building rapport means finding the strategies and approaches that build trust, break down walls of opposition and generate receptive moods.

■ *Focus on their agenda*

You are either building tension or you are building rapport. There is seldom any in-between. In all your interpersonal activities, people are being turned off or being turned on. I know people who are able to raise the tension level just by walking into a room. Their facial expression, posture, eye contact and stance express arrogance and belligerence. I know others who cause a warm glow and a feeling of friendship, respect and love when I meet them. They are sensitive, empathetic and thoughtful of the needs of others. Unfortunately, those that cause tension are not always aware of what is happening.

A classic example of this took place some years ago when my wife and I were upgrading our kitchen and decided we would like to have a new fridge and stove to make the job complete. After a number of visits to appliance stores we were still undecided. However I happened to be passing a well-known store one day and went in. I found just the thing I thought would please my wife and told the salesperson I would be back with her that evening.

careful to prepare a cheque as I felt sure we would buy. The salesperson met us with appropriate smile and handshake, and then proceeded to overwhelm my wife with details and facts, which were of no interest to her. She tried to get in a question relating to something that she was concerned about, but the salesperson did not even hear her. He was too busy focussing on his own agenda. It didn't take long for my wife to turn to me with a helpless look and say, "Don't we have an appointment that we have to get to in 15 minutes?" We walked out of the store with the cheque in my pocket. Now there was a salesman who was an expert at building tension. He never listened, never asked any questions, never really acknowledged my wife. He lost the sale. My guess is that he probably loses them regularly.

■ Remember names forever

Using a person's name really helps. When people call me by my name something stirs inside of me. The problem is that they don't do it very often. I can count on the fingers of one hand when participants in my seminars called me by my name, despite the fact I wore it on my lapel, and I had it on the board. There just seems to be a reluctance to say "Vince." On the other hand, I constantly call them by their names.

At an office I visit frequently, a lady teased me that I had forgotten her name, so I made a commitment to myself to remember it forever. Next time I visited her office I made a point to pass by her desk and say "Hi Dorothy." She bloomed! Just remembering her name seemed to make the world of difference to her.

How do you remember names? Easy! First, you must want to remember, because it takes energy. Once you make up your mind you want to remember someone's name, then "put another head" on them. Take the name of the person you want to remember, and associate it with someone you know well. Every time you look at the new person, "see" the person you know well. For instance, if you have just been introduced to Trevor King, search your memory for a Trevor you know well. Then visualize the "old" Trevor with a crown, sitting on a royal throne. Take the "old" Trevor's head and imaginatively put it on Trevor King. Every time you see Trevor King you will remember the picture and his name. After a short while the new person's name will become internalized even without association. I use this system quite often in seminars with up to 25 participants. It might take me half an hour to get the names straight, and then I am all right for the rest of the day. There are other memory strategies that you might like to explore at your library.

■ *Don't be the expert*

Let me tell you something else I have found out. It doesn't always pay to act like the expert. Too much confidence and independence is counter productive. I find that if I act like I need help (when I really do) I'll nearly always get it. Now let's get something clear. If we use this as a manipulative tool, it's not going to work. Most people can tell a fake at a distance. If you try to get something for nothing, try to take advantage of people, or use proven techniques to get more than your fair share, you will be found out for what you are. Remember, "What you are shouts so loud that I can't hear what you are saying."

Listen more than you talk

If you listen more than you talk you are on your way to being a great persuader. That sounds strange doesn't it? Bet you always thought a good talker is a good persuader. Wrong! Do you know that the best salespersons are the best listeners? Tom Hopkins, author of **How to Master the Art of Selling**, and North America's greatest sales trainer, told us in a seminar, "You listen yourself into a sale far faster than you talk yourself into it." Too much talking turns people off. It creates tension and lowers the level of rapport. Learn to listen and become a great persuader (more on this in Chapter 5).

Learn to ask questions

Asking questions is one of the oldest tools of persuasion. The reason is simple. It gets people talking, and people love to talk.

One of the most destructive things in relationships, confirmed by millions of divorces, broken partnerships and failed friendships, is the complaint that nobody listens. We try to impress others by who we are, and we do this by telling them. Over and over again we tell them about our achievements and our dreams. While we are doing this, other people lose their chance to tell of their achievements. Frustration sets in. By and by they look for other audiences who are more receptive to their needs. Learn to ask questions -- sincere questions, born out of a genuine interest in people. Find out what makes them tick, and as they talk they will be impressed with you. Not because of your speaking ability, but because of your ability to listen and make it easy for them to talk.

■ *Be specific when you compliment*

Giving compliments is a tool you need to handle very carefully. If you use it carelessly, it could hurt you badly. Insincere compliments are worse than no compliments at all. If you deal in flattery, people will avoid you like the plague. Here is a safe way to give compliments. Always be specific about what you are admiring. Also, it might be better to do it exactly when it happens. You have more credibility then.

There is a telephone operator I often speak to as I do business with the company she works with. Just recently I had to call her company at least five times during the course of one day. It just seemed Janet was waiting on my call every time, as the telephone was answered almost immediately. On the fifth call I said to her, "Janet, I would like to speak to Maurice, but just before you put me through, let me say a word to you. I want to congratulate you on the way you answer the phone. I know how busy you can get some times on the switch-board, yet all my calls today were answered almost instantaneously. And what a cheerful voice you have. It's just a pleasure to call your company. Just wanted to say that to you, Janet. Would you put me through to Maurice now." Her response? "Well, thank you," she said, "I feel good about that, and as you know, I enjoy my job." I don't think Janet felt I was manipulating her. After all, the evidence was there and she knew it.

■ *Give a little gift*

Give something away. It doesn't have to be an expensive gift. Perhaps just a business card or a pen. My wife taught me that. When we are visiting friends, she must take something along. It's such a priority with her that it sometimes is frustrating. We will be all dressed and ready to go to visit John and Laurie. Like any other family, we are running a little late at this time. Then Hyce says, "We must stop at the drug store. I would like to find a gift." My response? "We just don't have time dear. We are already late." Then the clincher, "Well, I'm not going without a little gift."

Get in the habit of always thinking of what you can give to people. I give away "A" cards, which are reinforcing tools to help remind you of some commitment you have made to yourself. I have friends that give away pens. Some give books.

■ *Lighten up and laugh*

Have fun when you meet people. I'm thinking of a
friend of mine now. He is a "fun" person. You are
never long in his company until he has you laughing.
Some people are so serious they get you down.
Laugh a little. Lighten up.

Do you know that laughing can actually improve
your health? You should read Norman Cousins'
book: **The Anatomy of an Illness.** In his book,
Cousins described a period in his life when he
suffered a serious illness. His doctors did not hold
out much hope for him surviving. Cousins analysed
the period preceding his illness and concluded that
stress and worry had a lot to do with him getting
sick. He calculated that if stress and worry had
brought on his illness, then perhaps the opposite
emotions would cure him. He then proceeded to
"laugh" himself to health. He obtained movies, read
books, had people visit him who would make him
laugh. He laughed until it hurt. Guess what? He
began to improve! Eventually he regained complete
health and passed on his findings in a remarkable
book from which the medical profession likes to
quote. Have you had your laugh today? It just
might save your life.

All of us have a streak of humour in us. Some, of
course, more than others. We love to be in the
company of those who are able to make us laugh

and have fun. Why not try a little of it yourself. Practice being more fun-oriented. Let people remember you as a person who loves to laugh and see the funny side of things. A dull, morose, sarcastic and complaining kind of person leaves us feeling discouraged.

That was the kind of person Gerry was. The moment he landed at our house he would start complaining. The traffic was awful, and the house was hard to find, and he wasn't feeling well, and it looked as if it was going to rain. Then he would launch into his latest confrontation at the office. Some fine details on how he was being taken advantage of and how he didn't get the promotion he was due. Some specifics on how partial and unfair his manager was, and then finally some plans on taking his company to court. He eventually did too and lost! Gerry's visits were always anticipated with great apprehension. We knew we were in for a day or two of whining, complaining and worry. How different his wife was though. She always found something to laugh about. Truly a remarkable person. Despite all the dark clouds, she could always find a silver lining. We all loved her.

■ *Use equality language*

Use equality language. Has someone ever asked you who you worked for? Were you ever referred to as a subordinate? Did anybody ever say you were blue collar? We all have important jobs. We are all a part of making things work well, and if we didn't do our job, things would not work very well. Wherever you are you are important. We need to recognize this and reflect it in our language. We don't work for anyone, we work with someone. We are not subordinate to anyone, but we might report to someone in the chain of command to keep things organized and coordinated. If we are white collar, we wouldn't have a job without blue collars. So let's start recognizing that some of these words are demeaning and make people feel less than what they are. Whenever I hear somebody say "my secretary" it makes me cringe inside. I get a mental picture of someone who is at the beck and call of an insensitive boss. "Get my coffee" or "I need this letter." I get a much better feeling when I am introduced to a person as, "John helps me" or "Mary is my assistant." Maybe it is just semantics, but it certainly helps to build a better climate with a greater level of rapport.

■ *Respect personal space*

Respect personal space. This is a fun one and always brings to mind a friend of mine I used to meet quite often in the supermarket on a Friday evening. He would rush over to me, greeting me in an enthusiastic way. Then as we talked he would get closer and closer. At times I would almost wonder if our noses would touch. I would begin to back pedal, but he would just follow through and keep talking. Although he was a good friend and I regarded his behaviour in a humorous way, it did make me a little uncomfortable. With a stranger exhibiting the same behaviour, I would have been extremely uncomfortable.

If you are meeting someone for the first time, be aware of their personal space. If you invade it, the person will become preoccupied and will probably not even hear what you are saying. Some cultures tend to be more aware of personal space than others. In North America, appropriate space for a first time meeting is in the area of two feet. Anything less than that makes the average person begin to feel uncomfortable. Other cultures are less sensitive and allow much closer proximity even for initial meetings.

Of course, if the relationship is a friendship, or love mate or spouse, then all rules go out the window. Then you use your own judgement and you take your chances. Just be careful though of your judgement. A few years ago I thought that my friendship with Carol allowed for a discreet embrace and kiss on the cheek when we met. Unfortunately she didn't think so, and I went through the embarrassing experience of being gently evaded, as I signaled my intent. It was not until years after that Carol decided it appropriate for that kind of invasion of her personal space. At that time, she made the advance, and of course I responded enthusiastically.

People signal their preference for how they want to be treated. Even in the matter of shaking hands, it is sometimes advisable to watch for the lead someone is giving you. Don't force people to do what they don't want to do. Be respectful of people's personal space, follow their lead for the kind of greeting they like, and you will be off to a good start.

19 Strategies that build Rapport

- Ask for help
- Don't depend on words only
- Dress for success
- Smile and change the climate
- Hold your head high
- Speak with your eyes
- Warm-up your handshake
- Add vitality to your voice
- Bridge the gap with sincerity
- Make your message congruent
- Give respect and empathy
- Focus on their agenda
- Remember names forever
- Don't be the expert

- Be specific when you compliment
- Give a little gift
- Lighten up and laugh
- Use equality language
- Respect personal space

Chapter 5

18 KEYS TO LISTENING
THAT STRENGTHEN RELATIONSHIPS
AND BUILD TRUST

Is somebody looking for you?

If you are a good listener, somebody is looking for
you. A lot of people may be looking for you right
now! Friends are chosen by their capacity to listen.

Close your eyes and think of the two best friends
you have. Are they good listeners? Usually when I
ask that question in seminars the answer is "yes."
Certainly I am drawn to the people that listen well.
I tend to avoid people that are poor listeners. You
probably are the same way. And so are a lot of
people out there. Listeners are powerful persuaders,
because they impact our attitudes and make us
more receptive. It stands to reason that if someone
listens to you, you will tend to want to listen to
them.

Randy is a powerful talker. He talks so much that
people try to avoid him. He has an opinion on
everything, and as far as he is concerned, his
opinion is always right. He knows the prescription
for every ailment, the solution to every business
problem, and the final answer to the woes of the
world. He is absolute in his conviction that his
views are right. He wearies people with his constant

refrain, "This is what you should do." After a while
they begin to shun him. They become smothered
with the constant one-way communication. Randy is
so insensitive he never sees what is happening, and
if he sees, he doesn't care.

Friendship is not built on one-way communication.
We all want to be listened to at some time, so we
tend to seek out those people willing to give us an
ear. There are thousands of lonely people right now
looking for someone to listen to them. If you want
to have a meaningful relationship, it's really quite
simple.   Establish yourself as a good listener. Ask
questions and show sincere interest in the other
person. You'll soon have to retreat from the throng
of people that come knocking at your door. Yes,
someone is looking for you, if you only learn the
techniques of good listening.

The great persuader

When we think of communication we tend to think
of a good talker. Communication for most people is
sending the message and doing it well. Traditionally,
the more we could talk, the better we were at
communicating. Up until recently, there were very
few courses on listening, but there was always a
plethora of workshops, seminars and courses on
speaking. The libraries overflow with books on **How
to Speak Confidently** or **Powerful Presentations**
and other similar titles. Very little on how listening
makes you a great persuader.

■ *Communicate in both directions*

A question on one of my project sheets never fails to prompt some interesting discussion: "It has been said that we have a greater effect on people by the way we listen than by the way we talk. How do you feel about that?" After some in-depth discussion, the participants usually conclude that both listening and talking have their place, and the proportion is close to 50:50. Sure there are times when talking is more important than listening, but there are also many times when listening is more important than talking.

Good communication goes both ways. It can hardly be said better than Chrysler Chairman Lee Iacocca's view: "I only wish I could find an institute that teaches people how to listen. After all a good manager needs to listen at least as much as he needs to talk. Too many people fail to realise that real communication goes in both directions." If you ever hope to influence and persuade, you must learn to listen. Take an interest in other people and you will find that they will be more inclined to take an interest in you. Be a two-way communicator.

■ *Don't advise, criticize or judge*

One time I flew 5000 miles just to talk to someone. I knew that person would listen to me and make me feel better.

Sometimes we have those experiences and we are glad for those people who have learned the art of listening, and so can relieve the stress, discouragement and frustration that we experience at times. We just want to "unload" to someone. No advice, no instructions, no answers, just a chance to articulate our deep feelings and find ourselves again. How kind a good listener seems at times like that. She is empathetic, putting herself into our place, knowing that all we need is understanding. It takes a lot of control to refrain from jumping in and offering advice, which is neither wanted nor needed at that time.

There's a beautiful story about Abraham Lincoln during the historic years of the Civil War. Burdened down with the awesome decisions of that tragic war, Lincoln sent for an old friend from his days in the backwoods of Illinois. When the old man arrived, Lincoln talked...and talked and talked. The old man listened...and then listened again! All the worry and care and frustration and suffering caused by the war just poured out. As Lincoln talked to this empathetic listener, he began to see the answers to some of the questions and challenges he faced. At the end of the day he thanked the old man for his help and sent him back to Illinois. He, the old man, probably knew that he had been more help than all the sophisticated advisers, counsellors and consultants that Lincoln had too many of.

Sometimes the answers to big problems are very simple. Like listening to people, and in that way, helping them find their own answers.

Some years ago, a worried and concerned man came to me after a seminar and asked for my help. He then proceeded to tell a tragic story of his failing marriage, his concern for the children and the awful question of a looming divorce. He asked me what he should do. I felt helpless before such a challenge. I asked questions. I let him talk and helped him to think through some of the questions he had to face. I watched as he began to find his own answers, and I saw him go away with a determination to follow a decision he had made. The sequel to this story is that I meet this man quite often at association meetings and other events. He never fails to come over and give me a great big hug and thank me again for what I did for him. Me do something for him? All I did was listen and ask some questions that got him thinking. Of course that taught me a profound lesson. I never try to find answers for others. I try to ask them the right questions that help them to find their own answers.

Some thousands of years ago, a great leader found the secret of helping people solve their own problems. He found that he could do this by asking the right kinds of questions. Unfortunately, he was too far ahead of his time, so they killed him. His name was Socrates, and today the Socratic method is a system of asking questions for results.

You can do so much for people as a good listener. There are lonely people, people with back breaking problems, people with broken hearts, and people burdened down with sorrow. Just listening to them with feeling and with care will help them feel so much better. You will be appreciated, respected and revered, and the result is that you will have influence with these people. Imagine the kind of trust these people will have in you. Imagine the kind of power you will have with them. They will want to do the things you ask them to do.

Open minds build trust and respect

One of the greatest enemies of good listening is the narrow view we retain of leadership. Maybe it came from the long tradition of kings and emperors and dictators and usurpers. We tend to think of leadership as someone up there at the front, giving the orders, leading the way and making the decisions. In that kind of leader, listening has no place. Many of us still see listening in a leader as a weakness and a factor that will eventually cause failure. How wrong!

The great leaders today in business, politics and religion are people that listen. Leaders that are strong enough in their own self esteem that they can entertain the ideas and opinions of others. They don't necessarily have to be guided by those opinions, but they recognise the importance of listening. And quite often an idea appears that might take them off the course they are on and set them on a new course. Today's leaders have the courage to test their own ideas against the ideas of others. Some of the failed leaders today are simply the result of going against that trend. They are selective listeners. They hear what they want to hear. They close their ears to the truth. They lack the courage to hear the things contrary to their own views.

■ *Use ear and heart to heal and help*

Some years ago I had the good fortune to work with a group of people who taught me an unforgettable lesson about listening. I call it the *critical factor* in listening. If you have this quality, you will be in demand among friends and business acquaintances. You will be an influencer and a persuader.

I had been talking to a group of people some of whom were from Japan. The focus of discussion was on listening and, during one of the coffee breaks, one of the Japanese participants asked me a question. "Have you ever seen *listening* written in Japanese?" I replied that I had never seen listening written in Japanese and wondered why he had asked. His reply was that some of the things I had been saying about listening were very closely related to the way that listening was written in the Japanese language.

My curiosity was now aroused, and I asked him to write the word "listening" in Japanese for me. This is what he wrote:

What he told me about these symbols was so simple but so profound I have been speaking about it ever since. He said, "In the English language you build words by putting different letters of your alphabet together to build the desired word. In Japanese, and indeed all of the Oriental languages, we take symbols and build words. Now this word *listening* in Japanese is made up of two symbols. The first symbol means *the ear,* suggesting that if you are going to listen you should use your ear. The other symbol means *the heart,* suggesting that good listening means the heart has to be involved.(see page 79)

Too many of us tend to use the "mechanics" of listening without having that *critical factor.* We give good eye contact, we are careful never to interrupt, we give feedback and avoid jumping to conclusions. But deep inside, we really don't care! Good listening is as much the use of the heart as it is the use of the ear.

How many times have you had somebody listen to you and although they might have been giving the appropriate eye contact, there was the awful realization that they really didn't care. They were fulfilling their roles as managers, or supervisors or perhaps even friends by listening to you. But you knew that they had no heart.

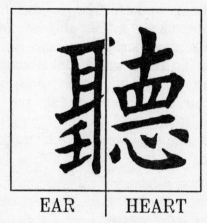

EAR | HEART

Not so long ago a participant at a seminar shared with me during the lunch period a problem he had. It was a big problem, and I was not about to try to provide an answer. But I cared! The result was that he was able to articulate his problem and, in doing so, began to understand it better and see some possible options. You can do that for your friends and acquaintances too.

■ *Walk in their shoes, sit in their chairs*

We don't need to go to the Japanese language to find the *critical factor.* We have the equivalent in an English word we are all familiar with. That word is *empathy,* and it means "putting yourself in another person's place" or, as the native Canadians say, "walking in another person's mocassins." Psychologist Carl Rogers says it eloquently as he describes real communication. He says, "It means to see the expressed idea and attitude from the other person's point of view, to sense how it feels to them and to achieve their frame of reference in regard to what they are talking about." One of the high achievements of listening is to be able to get right into other people's skins and understand where they are coming from. To really get a look through their eyes at the perspective that they are expressing. Then and only then can we understand all the factors that prompt them to say and do the things they say and do. Without empathy we are "one track," insensitive and stubborn.

■ *Shut up and grow*

Some people never change. Some people never grow. Some people never understand the tremendous potential they have as human beings. They go on year after year, talking, talking, talking, and never listen long enough to hear and understand that they are holding themselves back.

Gloria is a good example of a no-growth experience. I met her years ago when we were asked to get together to talk about a project we might do jointly. My first contact with Gloria was on the telephone. She monopolized the conversation and hardly allowed me a chance to explain who I was, my area of expertise, and how I would like to approach the assignment. When we met, Gloria was no different. I had to sit and listen to a long oration about her accomplishments, the best way to approach our assignment and what the result would likely be. She quickly confirmed in my mind that she was going to be a difficult person to work with, and I was not looking forward to the assignment.

The project did not materialize. Problems developed because of Gloria's attitude and style and the client detected that it was not a good working relationship. The point to be made is that Gloria lost a good opportunity to get exposure and enhance her image and business potential. Now many years later, she is still not listening and is still struggling to keep her business going. She has not stopped long enough to listen to what people are saying to her. She has not heard the message, "Gloria, you talk too much. Stop for a moment and listen to what people are trying to tell you." Have you ever met anyone like that? Someone who you feel you could just sit down in a chair and shout into their ear, "Listen, you fool! You are turning people off, and it's causing you to fail. You are not growing, because you are not listening."

Listening is one of the greatest educators that we have as human beings. I have a friend whose life was changed through listening. The way he tells it is that he was opinionated, narrow and obtuse. There was no room for any other perspectives or points of view but his own. His listening was a superficial exercise. He heard the words, but those words never really penetrated into his consciousness and impacted his thinking. He was too locked into his own way of thinking. His mindset was too powerful for anything to break through. He was a prisoner to biases, prejudices and narrow thinking.

Then he got involved with an organization where he had to sit and listen to speeches and presentations that quite often represented views and perspectives opposite to his. Slowly at first, and then with gathering momentum he began to pay attention to some of the views being expressed. One day it dawned on him that he might not have all the answers. He began to suspect that perhaps there were other legitimate views besides his. In religion, politics and business, there were other ways that were workable and viable. Suddenly new horizons opened up to him. A whole new world was created for him. Life became a different experience. All because of learning how to listen.

■ *Learn from everyone*

We can learn from the world's biggest fool! If all we get is an insight into the things that we should not do, and the perspectives we want to avoid, we have learned from that person. I have been to presentations that I have not enjoyed and performances that were unrewarding. Was the time wasted? No! I learned that here is a style I want to avoid, a way of thinking that does not work. We learn new lessons from the wise and from the foolish. Give everyone a chance to express himself.

■ *Listen twice as much as you talk*

Perhaps there is a message in the fact that we have two ears, two eyes and one mouth. Could that be interpreted to mean that we should be hearing and seeing twice as much as we talk? Some people go through life preaching, ordering and pontificating on their opinions. What happens is that they get so locked into their own way of seeing things that they become narrow and prejudiced. Their constant talking does not allow them to get enough information to help them see the error of their ways. Unless they begin to lend some time to listening and thinking, they will forever remain where they are. They are locked into their own world, unaware of the way others see them, isolated and perhaps even avoided by those who could really help them.

■ *Monitor yourself*

If you want to start a new day in your life, try listening. Start monitoring yourself and forcing yourself to listen to even the youngest child. Start asking questions. Become the Socrates of your family or your company. Ask the questions that will begin to tell you what others really think. Challenge yourself to learn what drives the behaviour of those around you. Learn the deep root causes that result in the behaviour expressed by friends, business acquaintances and others. You may find as a result that your life will be changed. Changed for the better. You'll feel more rewarded, satisfied and serene just because you listened.

■ *Give positive eye contact*

Marion is a young woman who came to one of my seminars recently. I noticed her immediately because of her complete lack of eye contact. In casual conversation she avoided my eyes completely. She showed real discomfort as we talked. She shifted her eyes from the floor to her dress, fleetingly to my shoulder area and then back to the floor. I couldn't help feeling that here was a young lady almost void of self-confidence.   The lack of eye contact made me feel she was not listening. Her whole demeanor, highlighted by the avoidance of eye contact made me feel that real communication had been thwarted.

Good eye contact does not mean that we stare people down and make them uncomfortable. Good listeners exhibit a relaxed and comfortable eye contact that suggests, "I am interested in what you have to say. Please keep talking. I like you." At times, move your eyes to other areas such as the gestures the talker might be making. Temper your eye contact with glances to other appropriate points, especially if you see that continuous eye contact makes the other party uncomfortable.

■ *Acknowledge what you heard*

Want to let the talker know you are a good listener? Then make sure to repeat the words you just heard. Not every time. Not slavishly and obviously, but choosing the appropriate time, paraphrase and summarize what the talker has said. It's a compliment to the speaker when you repeat what she said. It means that you heard and understood. It means that you took the time to concentrate and hear what she said. It also does something else! It clarifies what is being said and ensures that misunderstanding does not develop.

A good way to be sure that you understood what someone said, is to repeat it. Phrases such as, "let me see if I understand what you said. This is what I heard..." Or, "What I hear you saying is that ..." This kind of careful listening ensures understanding, which of course is the object of communication. Some might object that this kind of feedback takes time. It certainly does, but over the long haul it saves time and quite often money. When we understand a person we avoid misunderstandings, mistakes, frustration and tension.

■ *Take some notes*

A few days ago I met with a committee to discuss a program I was customizing for the company. I was impressed and pleased to notice that most of the committee members had paper and pencil in hand as we started the meeting. That was a signal to me that they regarded our discussion as important. It gave me a feeling of importance and raised my level of motivation for the meeting.

Taking notes while listening is a compliment to the speaker and should be encouraged. Sometimes, because of the particular circumstance, you might like to ask permission. If the meeting is a one-on-one event, you might say, "do you mind if I take some notes to ensure that I don't forget any of our discussion?" In most instances the speaker will be flattered you are going to take the time to write down what he says. Take short form notes. Lengthy writing where eye contact is lost is not recommended. A word or two will help to bring back the idea or concept discussed. Sometimes just a number is all that is required. Just enough to help you make more elaborate notes after the meeting when you are reviewing and summarizing the discussion.

Good listening means that you also summarize the result of your discussion afterward. Carry a pad and pencil at all times so that following a conversation you can make notes. To trust your memory is not good business. One quote I heard in my teenage years is a good adage to follow: "The palest ink is better than the most retentive memory." Credit the Chinese with that one. It is wisdom that comes from the sages of an old and wise civilization. It certainly has helped me through the years. You don't forget too much when you have it on paper.

A more modern sage in the person of Lee Iacocca also said: "....the moment you write something down it immediately and dramatically increases the potential for it happening." Want to achieve more? Get into the habit of writing things down, especially the advice that others give you.

■ *Don't interrupt*

Ever feel frustrated when you want to tell a story and someone keeps telling it for you? I know a young couple who are a dramatic example of what I call the "interrupt syndrome." As soon as the husband starts to tell his story from his own experience, his wife jumps in to tell it for him. This is something that he experienced himself. She wasn't there! But she takes over the telling of the story. What does he do? Shuts up and lets her tell it. But he also shows by his body language that he is frustrated and angry at the insensitivity. He is a patient man, and of course that is the only reason why it happens. I know another couple where it's the husband who always takes over the telling of the story. Not only is this poor listening, but it's downright rude. It exhibits a lack of self control and a lack of empathy for the other person. It can only breed a poor relationship over the long haul, or perhaps force the other partner into the role of wall flower or silent partner.

One of the factors that sponsor better relationships and encourage agreement is the art of listening people out. Don't interrupt! Listen to what the other party has to say and then respond. It says in subtle tones, "What you have to say is important, and I want to hear all of it." It improves the climate for negotiation and builds a more receptive attitude on the part of others.

What happens when a person talks too much and just monopolizes the time? Then might be the time to do some positive interrupting. If the speaker takes an unreasonable amount of time to present her side of the story, you might like to suggest that you have listened and now it is your time to talk. After having listened, it is the unreasonable person that would not reciprocate and provide time for you to talk. If a person refuses this obligation, you might like to question if you should be talking to her in the first place.

■ *A nod and a smile helps the speaker*

A few days ago I was talking to my good friend Tom on the telephone. He likes to call me on his car phone. Trouble is sometimes he gets into a location where reception on car phones is poor and his voice disappears on me. This day we were having a lively conversation, and after a comment by me I waited on his response. No answer! "Tom," I said, "are you there?" No answer! "Tom," I literally shouted into the phone, "are you there?" "Oh yes, I'm just thinking," he said. Ever get the feeling while you are talking to someone that they are "just thinking," and not about what you are talking about?

Good communication is giving those little nuances and signals that say we are listening and listening very carefully. Sometimes a certain look in the eye, or a raised eyebrow signaling surprise, or perhaps a question. More often a movement of the head that says "Yes, I hear you." Even more positive is saying "right, right" to signal agreement. It is in our interest to help the other party communicate to the best of his ability, and positive responses certainly help in that area. Lack of responses tend to shut a person down and make him uncommunicative.

One of my most memorable experiences was while trying to talk to a group of people who gave no positive responses. I had been asked to speak to a group of employees at lunch in their cafeteria. What I did not know was that the employees had not been told there would be a speaker, and their lunch time was to be monopolized by a promotion. They signaled their displeasure by totally ignoring me. No eye contact, no acknowledgement of my presence, no comment. Actually they continued eating and conversing among themselves as if I didn't exist. It was a harrowing experience. It was all I could do to keep my thoughts together and make sense to myself. I never want to do that again. A dramatic example of what we do to people when we do not give them some kind of acknowledgement through body language and short comments that we are listening.

■ *Don't jump ahead of the speaker*

"I know what you are going to say." How many times have you been guilty of saying that? Perhaps not out loud, but mentally. We jump ahead of the speaker and form opinions of what he is going to say long before it is said. Sometimes we don't hear what the speaker said because we have already formed an opinion and so are guilty of selective listening.

Selective listening is the kind of listening that lets us hear what we want to hear. We have already formed an opinion and we hear the things that support this pre-formed opinion. This happens very easily and subtly. We all have biases and prejudices, pre-formed concepts which have developed into strong belief patterns in our minds. When we hear the words of others, we tend to manipulate the words into a format that says the things we want to hear.

How do we overcome this natural, human tendency? By listening with an open mind. Easier said than done! Slow down your mental machine, and hold back the conclusions you come to as the other party is speaking. What is the point they are making? What is the rationale they are providing to support that point? If a person is introducing points that are not being supported, then ask for the evidence that relates to the particular point.

Poor thinking is an acceptance of ideas and concepts that have no support by experience in the real world. A good listener takes her time. Listen the speaker out, then analyse what has been said through feedback and questions. "What do you mean when you say..?" "Is this what you mean when you say...?" "What I hear you saying is..." This is effective analysis and clear thinking. With this kind of approach you will separate the biases and prejudices from the facts and come a little closer to the truth. Instead of jumping to false conclusions, you will arrive safely at sensible answers.

■ *Concentrate and ignore distractions*

Years ago we were vacationing in New Brunswick. We were in the city of St. John for the celebration of the landing of The Loyalists. It was a moving spectacle. Prime Minister John Diefenbaker was there to celebrate with the city. I'll never forget being close to Mr. Diefenbaker and seeing just how he treated the people who were literally mobbing him. He gave each person he spoke to, his absolute and complete attention. Despite all the excitement and confusion going on around him, he kept his cool and was relaxed and calm. As he spoke to person after person, he gave them full eye contact and spoke directly to them for the time he spent with them. He gave each person he spoke to about 20 - 30 seconds of his time. The mark of a great listener is the ability to shut out all distractions and give full and complete attention to the person speaking.

Poor listeners tend to lose concentration and attend to incidental interruptions such as a fellow employee walking by, a magazine on a table or the clock on the wall. Active listening means focusing attention on the person speaking and shutting out all distractions. Sure it takes energy and discipline, but who said that listening was easy. We are told by experts that listening raises your blood pressure and causes your heart beat to increase. It takes energy and concentration and persistence and discipline. If it was easy we would all be experts at listening. Good listening takes knowledge and commitment.

■ *Ask appropriate questions*

The most successful salespersons are the ones who have learned the art of asking questions. Famous sales trainer Tom Hopkins, author of **How to Master the Art of Selling** said "...you listen yourself into a sale far faster than you talk yourself into one." Hopkins then went on to explain that selling is asking questions to find out the needs of the person and then trying to fill that need. Too often we think of selling as a conquering of the client's objections; a battle of words where the seller overwhelms the luckless client with facts, logic and the weight of argument.

Asking questions is the key to better communication and influencing people. Without knowing the particular needs of a person we are hard pressed to do anything for them. If we approach a person with just our own agenda and begin to force that agenda on them, we are not going to be very successful at persuading. The great majority of us think only of what we want to achieve, and then we try to bend others to our way of thinking. We do this through talking them down, or just sheer weight of words and argument. We do this without thinking of the needs, desires and objectives of the other side. Asking questions is the art of learning what motivates the other side. What is their agenda? When we have that kind of knowledge we are in the driver's seat. We can then begin to modify our own agendas to satisfy the other person's agenda. We get them on our side through satisfying some of their needs.

When we go into a negotiation or interpersonal activity, we quite often prepare carefully for the things we are going to say. Good sales persons, or negotiators or persuaders go further than that. They prepare a series of questions to reveal the hidden agendas of the other side. They are then in the enviable position of understanding where the other person is coming from and are able to do and say the things that win agreement.

■ *Practise talking less*

Most people that talk incessantly, frustrating their friends and acquaintances, are surprised when they are told they talk too much. We seldom see ourselves in the same way others see us. How can you know if you talk too much? Monitor yourself and measure the amount of air time that you take in a given conversation. After every interpersonal situation, analyse the event and try to calculate the proportion of the conversation you monopolised. Certainly there are times when it is necessary to carry most of the conversation. However, if you consistently monopolise events, your friends, co-workers and acquaintances will begin to see you as the kind of person that takes more than your fair share of the conversation. They will slowly begin to avoid you and eventually, if you do not take the hint, begin to shun you. Incessant talkers are not welcome by the average person, merely tolerated.

Sometimes just the act of silence tends to lend an aura of confidence, credibility and wisdom. We have all heard of strong, silent people who act as role models for others. Some good advice came from Winston Churchill concerning talking less: "...better to keep your mouth shut, than open it and reveal the emptiness of mind." Another factor worth considering is that while you are talking you are not learning. If we spend all our time pontificating and preaching our own doctrine, we will never hear the other doctrines which may have something to teach us.

Talking less is also an expression of confidence. Most incessant talkers are prompted by a feeling of "lack," which they tend to respond to by incessant talk. They try to shore up their poor self-image by talking about themselves and promoting their achievements.

Far more respect is extended to people who are careful about revealing their achievements, and who express attitudes of control and confidence.

■ *Follow through with action*

You can take all the notes you want, ask lots of questions and give positive responses, but if you don't follow through and do something about what is being said, you will be branded as a poor listener. People are looking for more than an intellectual and courteous response to the things they are saying to you. They are looking for action. Perhaps more than anywhere else, this is where the story of good listening is told.

Ron is in his manager's office. He is telling him about a new procedure the night shift discovered while installing the die in the stamping equipment. Ron is excited about his discovery, and explains how much time the new idea will save. "This will be a big saving for the company in man hours and material," he says. His manager makes some notes and thanks Ron for his interest and enthusiasm.

A few days go by and Ron wonders what has happened. He had expected his manager would have the new idea in operation by the next day. But maybe his manager is busy and will get to the changes in a few more days. A few weeks go by and Ron begins to suspect that nothing will happen. After all wasn't that what happened last year when Rupert Gray made a suggestion to improve the process of ordering inventory? As the weeks grow into months and Ron hears nothing about his cost-saving suggestion, he joins his colleagues who long ago learned the refrain, "Nobody listens to us around here." They smile at Ron as he joins them for lunch, and one of them comments sarcastically, "Did the big boss get to you yet Ron?" Others are a little kinder and say, "We told you so, Ron. That's the way the system works." Chalk up another positive, caring and interested employee won over to the negative, discouraged and frustrated group.

Not every idea is a good idea. Some are worthless, unrealistic and "off the wall." However, every idea should get a response. Listening is showing that we heard and we did something about it. The Iacocca philosophy is worth mentioning again: "...if you never get back to the guy he will never give you another idea."

Really, if Ron's idea was unrealistic, all that was needed was a short meeting explaining his idea had some elements that were realistic and worthwhile, and some elements that tended to neutralize the positive factors. He needed an explanation that management did take the time to evaluate his idea and concluded that the long-term implications made his suggestion unworkable. "Ron we do appreciate your interest and time, and we hope this experience will demonstrate that management takes a real interest in all ideas and suggestions that are presented. We hope you will continue to examine and analyse our precedures and make further suggestions for improvement. Thanks again Ron for your interest." That will make for an interested and empowered person. His faith in the powers that be has been vindicated, and he can justify his efforts to his peers. Better still, of course, is if his suggestion proves to be viable and is implemented.

The final proof that you listened and listened well is that action results. The message I hear most often from managers, supervisors, line workers and support staff is that "nobody listens to me." The same message comes also from children, spouses and friends. That doesn't mean they weren't heard. That eye contact, feedback and caring were not evident. But it does mean that the result was *NOTHING.* A big, blank, empty, meaningless *NOTHING!* And when *NOTHING* is the result, it means listening did not take place.

18 Keys to Good Listening

- Communicate in both directions
- Don't advise, criticize or judge
- Use ear and heart to heal and help
- Walk in their shoes, sit in their chairs
- Shut up and grow
- Learn from everyone
- Listen twice as much as you talk
- Monitor yourself
- Give positive eye contact
- Acknowledge what you heard
- Take some notes
- Don't interrupt
- A nod and a smile helps the speaker
- Don't jump ahead of the speaker
- Concentrate and ignore distractions
- Ask appropriate questions
- Practise talking less
- Follow through with action

Chapter 6

12 WAYS TO DEAL
WITH DIFFICULT PEOPLE
AND NEGOTIATE WIN-WIN OUTCOMES

The Paradox of uniqueness

For me, Edgar was a very likable person. He was calm and friendly with an easy smile. Although he had a wide knowledge of the subject we were discussing at our first meeting, he had no airs and displayed no arrogance. We quickly adjusted to each other, and I rather enjoyed the comfortable way in which Edgar shared his knowledge with me. His intent was to persuade me to make some investments through his company. I found myself being drawn towards him and beginning to trust him, as well as appreciating the wealth of knowledge he had about the investment field.

On the other hand, my partner had an entirely different response to Edgar. For him, Edgar was a little too "slick." He talked too much and was obviously manipulating us into moving our investments into his reach.

Here was a dramatic demonstration of how two people can look at the same person or situation and react in entirely different ways. Each of us drew differing conclusions because of a complex number of factors. We viewed the same situation or behaviour through the screens of our past experience and conditioning, our values, attitudes and belief systems.

This combination of conditioning, values, attitudes and belief systems is what makes each of us a unique person. No one else, not even identical twins, will have the exact combination of these factors. Each of us is a world onto ourselves, interpreting behaviours and circumstances in different ways.

However, it is this quality of uniqueness more than any other factor that causes others to be difficult for us. We have our own way of looking at the world and the things that happen. We have our own guidelines about how people should act and behave. When they do not conform to the pattern we have chosen as "right," we label that behaviour as "wrong."

I know two brothers who have maintained a lifelong animosity and dislike for each other because they see things in different ways. They both are sure they are right. None of them are willing to compromise in any way. One believes in "telling it as it is." People should be told when they are wrong. The other believes in a more lenient and tolerant view. Be patient and understand that mistakes will be made. Give people a chance to make some mistakes and be kinder to them. There seems to be no meeting place, no common ground. Each is a difficult person for the other, because each is an inflexible person, adamant in his own way of seeing the world, absolutely convinced his way is the only "right" way.

We live in different worlds

It is easy to understand that people who live in Iraq live in a different world from we who live in North America. It is not so easy to grasp that you live in a different world from the people you live and work with. You live in a different world from people in your own family. Even your spouse finds it difficult at times to enter your world and understand the behaviour that your particular background, culture, values, attitudes and emotions prompt you to indulge in.

This unique quality that we possess can be both a wonderful gift and a curse. On the one hand we are blessed with the opportunity of being someone entirely different from others, but on the other hand, our uniqueness makes it hard to understand others. It gets worse too! Sometimes we are very far apart. Some people are friendly, trusting and open, while others are suspicious and cautious of others. The perspectives and outlook from these two vantage points are so different that in most instances it will be impossible for compromise to be reached. It literally would be like two people on either side of the planet trying to communicate with each other. Their views are so removed, that there is no place for understanding. They are in effect, worlds apart.

Those who have acquired the art of influence and persuasion are those who understand this phenomenon of uniqueness. They are sensitive to the differing perspectives every human being will have because of his or her background and conditioning influences. They are aware that their own backgrounds and conditioning influences have shaped opinions that make them see things quite differently from anyone else. With this understanding, they are able to be tolerant and patient with the uniqueness of others. They are able to adjust to the extreme viewpoints others display. They have that valuable quality of flexibility which allows them to adjust to and cope with "difficult" behaviour.

The roots of behavioural patterns

As discussed in Chapter 3, cultural conditioning is a factor in forming some of our unique behavioural patterns. For instance, if you are from South America you probably like watching soccer. If you are from North America you will be a baseball fan. If you are from the British Isles you will enjoy watching and reading about cricket. You grew up with these activities and sports. It was ingrained in your psyche at a very young age that these were the things your particular culture enjoyed. You grew to accept this and adjusted your life-style to it.

We are always under the power of a conditioning factor. All of us are conditioned people and our behavioural trends are influenced by the culture and environment in which we grew up. If we see things enough times, and we are told over and over again they are acceptable and desirable, we will come to accept eventually that they are acceptable and desir-

able. The great majority of human beings go along
with what they see around them and are influenced
by their environment. Very few of us tend to challenge the things we are told and find our own way,
choosing our own path. Generally, Canadians grow
up like Canadians, Chinese grow up like Chinese,
Germans grow up like Germans, and on and on
and on.

Hereditary legacies are also a factor in forming
unique behavioural patterns. Take the case of Allan
who is an adopted child. Allan grew up in an
environment ideally conducive to success. His adoptive parents were highly educated people, possessing
high morals and playing a responsible role in their
community. Their natural children, outside of the
normal growing up problems, developed into responsible, likable adults. Not Allan! Although living in
the same environment as his adopted brothers and
sisters, he very early exhibited a mean streak.

He seemed intent on destroying the highly-respected
family name. He found undesirable friends who
helped him get in trouble with the law. He stole,
he lied, he ran away from home. Despite consul-
tations with psychologists, psychiatrists and doctors,
nothing really could be done for Allan. He spent
time in rehabilitation centres and reform organizations. The point of the story is that his adoptive
parents were warned during discussions that Allan's
background was questionable. Allan's mother and
father were irresponsible and had had problems
with the law.

Is it possible that some of Allan's difficult behaviour had been passed on in a hereditary sense? Was he in the power of a force psychologists and doctors were not a match for? Were there genes in his blood stream that contributed to the undesirable behaviour he exhibited? These are some of the questions we face when we look at difficult behaviour.

Discovering other worlds

Captain Picard travels out to other worlds every week on the popular show "Star Trek." He explores new civilizations and meets with new kinds of life and thought, as we sit back fascinated. The exploration of the worlds all around us - in the sense of other people - can be just as fascinating. Each of us is a complex world with values, ideas, belief systems and attitudes quite different from our peers.

The desire to explore these worlds is perhaps the first step towards becoming an expert at influencing and persuading others. It is in understanding the motives and hidden agendas of others that we begin to understand how they work, and what we can do to influence them in their thinking and subsequently their actions and behaviour.

The only way we could ever help Allan would be to get inside his world and understand the reasons why he behaved the way he did. We would have to journey with him through the maze of his desires, his emotions, his beliefs. We would have to try to understand why his immediate response to authority is distrust and antagonism. We would have to explore the areas where some trust could be built and how. We would have to let go of our own ideas of reality and common sense and, for a moment, allow ourselves to see through his eyes. In short, we would have to learn the fine art of empathy.

Allan's world is a formidable place. He is stalked constantly by undercover agents who want to capture him and put him in a correctional institution. He has to be alert to avoid being captured. His parents and relatives are all part of this imagined scenario. They are working together with the agents. Allan is the innocent but hunted party. His world is a world of constant war with the elements that are trying to destroy him. His thoughts are preoccupied with ways in which he can escape or avoid the apparent inevitable.

How can he win? How can he withstand the enemy? Right! He will hurt them and distract them by annoying them. He will attack them where he knows it will really hurt. He will destroy their good name by tempting the law and alerting the police. He will even break the law, and in so doing, bring notoriety to his family, and all those who have evil intentions towards him. Illogical and insane? Perhaps from our perspective but not so from the perspective of Allan. He can provide the rationale that satisfies him all the above is true. He can give instances to prove this scenario is indeed being worked out.

That is his world, and unless we can enter it and begin to understand where he is, we probably will never help Allan. He is of course an extreme case, bordering on schizophrenia. But it gives us an idea of the kind of scenario that takes place in the minds of those we label as difficult people. To begin to have any kind of influence, we must be able to put ourselves in their place and understand their kind of world. We must understand it makes perfect sense to them. All the unrealistic scenarios are to them the real truth.

If we can align with them and acknowledge their truth, we stand a chance of beginning to lead them out of the morass of negativity and of introducing them to the bright light of sanity, reality and compromise.

Our inner world is unique. We built it ourselves. We built it with the thoughts, values, beliefs, attitudes and motives we acquired over the years. Some of us have built a palace. The rooms are adorned with the furniture of love. The walls have pictures of patience and tolerance. The floor is covered with the carpet of understanding. There is a song of joy constantly playing in the halls of this beautiful edifice.

Other people live in quite a different dwelling. Their walls are made of hatred and suspicion. They look constantly through the window of despair and discouragement. For them, life is a mess and a tragedy. They could do without it. "Why the hell was I born?" Their world is despair, hopelessness and loss. Given the choice of building a beautiful world, they chose to build a fortress of war to defend themselves against an imaginary but ruthless enemy. Another difficult person has arrived!

■ Enter their world

When dealing with difficult people we enter their world by building trust and showing sincere interest by asking appropriate questions. Ask the kind of questions that indicate sincere interest: "How do you feel about what I said?" "Would you do it differently if you were deciding?" "What would you like to get out of this experience?" Involve the difficult person in discussion and acknowledge their objections. Failing to recognize their objections will only aggravate their antagonism and get them even further away from agreement.

A favourite story of mine concerning difficult people was shared with us in a seminar a few years ago. Margaret, a participant in the seminar, told us there was an employee in the organization in which she worked who was famous for being difficult. Everybody avoided him. They had learned over time it was pointless asking him to do anything outside of his job description. Sometimes it was even difficult to get him to do things included in his job description. He was so miserable and hard to get along with that fellow employees just avoided him and tried to do the best they could without him. The interesting part of the story though was this "difficult employee" would do almost anything for Margaret. Knowing this, some of her co-workers would sometimes go through her to get the job done. They would ask her to ask him, knowing that he would willingly respond to Margaret's requests.

Naturally our curiosity was aroused, and we wanted to know what special brand of persuasion Margaret used to get things done when nobody else could. Her answer was very simple. "I listen to him," she said. "I give him time, when nobody else seems to have time or desire to hear his concerns." A wonderful example of Margaret entering his world and empathizing with him. She was the only one that took time to understand this poor, lonely man. She showed interest and caring and he replied by responding to her every request in a positive way.

■ *Identify their style*

What kind of difficult person are you dealing with? One of the first challenges in dealing with a difficult person is to identify the particular behavioural style of the difficult person you are faced with. Is this person an "extreme dominant" or is she an "extreme cautious?"

Using the behavioural styles grid introduced in Chapter 4, we can establish in a fairly reliable way the significant factors that cause a person to be seen as difficult. Use the chart in Figure 1 on the next page and choose a difficult person and chart him or her on the horizontal axis. Take particular care in marking the degree to which this person is a "talkative" person or a "listening" person. If they are extreme in any of these areas, be sure to mark them towards the end of the axis.

Turning your attention to the vertical axis, again

FIGURE 1
BEHAVIOURAL STYLES

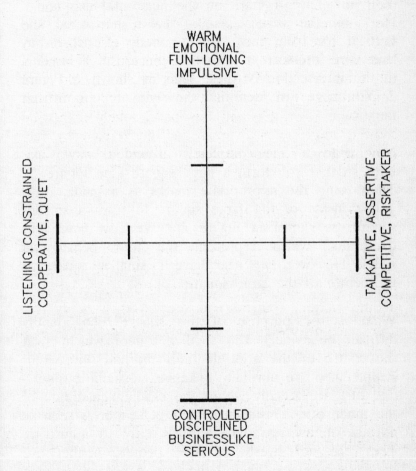

WARM
EMOTIONAL
FUN—LOVING
IMPULSIVE

LISTENING, CONSTRAINED
COOPERATIVE, QUIET

TALKATIVE, ASSERTIVE
COMPETITIVE, RISKTAKER

CONTROLLED
DISCIPLINED
BUSINESSLIKE
SERIOUS

mark the person, taking care to mark the degree to which this person is "warm and emotional" or "businesslike and serious," (For more detail on how to mark the horizontal and vertical axis on the behavioural style grid, please see the directions in

Chapter 4 on marking yourself and identifying your style).

You now have a mark on the horizontal axis and a mark on the vertical axis. Draw a horizontal and vertical line from each of these marks in such a way that they intersect at a certain point. Put a large X at the intersection of these lines as shown in Figure 2. You have just identified the style of your difficult person.

Now draw a line completely around the two axis lines so that you form a large square (see Figure 2). Then using the appropriate marks as a guide, draw a line inside of this large square to form a smaller square, as shown in Figure 2. We now have four quadrants, which represent the four behavioural styles. However, we also have a smaller square in the centre of the large square.

What is the purpose of this square? To identify difficult behaviour! The smaller square which is at the centre of the grid identifies "normal" behaviour. People who are normally talkative, normally business-like etc. are usually within the smaller quadrants of the inner box. This means their behaviour is seen as normal or average and is fairly easy to adjust to. They are not overly talkative people, neither are they overly quiet. Their behaviour is not so extreme that it causes undue tension.

The people outside of the inner box however, are another matter. They are extreme in their behaviour. They are the ones that are extremely talkative, extremely businesslike, extremely warm or extremely

FIGURE 2
DIFFICULT PERSON'S STYLE

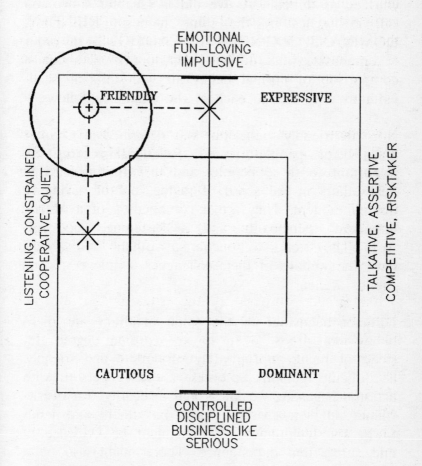

quiet. They form the group of people that are usually seen as difficult. Chances are you have marked your difficult person outside of the inner box and towards the extreme corner of one of the large quadrants.

If you have not, review the process and satisfy yourself that you have been objective in your assessment of the personality characteristics of the person you see as difficult. As we did in Chapter 4, we will call the styles by the same names: FRIENDLY, DOMINANT, EXPRESSIVE, CAUTIOUS. In order to emphasize what difficult behaviour is all about, a comparison of normal behaviour with difficult behaviour as it relates to each of the quadrants follows.

Normal "friendly" behaviour was described in Chapter 4 as being people-oriented. Relationships are very important to these people, and they find it hard to hurt others in the sense of saying "no" or having to discipline them. They are a combination of a "warm, impulsive" personality and a "listening, suportive" style. They tend to encourage others and always have the welfare of their colleagues, employees, and friends at heart.

Difficult behaviour in the same quadrant are these behavioural traits taken to an extreme degree. Instead of being appropriately supportive and friendly, a difficult person becomes a "yes" person with actions suggesting weakness and insecurity. An overly-friendly person lavishes praise on others and tends to be overly-optimistic. There might be evidence of uncertainty and dependence. There might also be a tendency to socialize a lot and appease, compromise and gloss over issues. This becomes frustrating for some people, particularly if they are in a different style quadrant. Imagine a dominant person, preoccupied with getting things done, dealing with a person who socialises a lot and does not deliver.

A dear friend of ours is a person I think of as a difficult person in the friendly quadrant. This person always wants to please. She is warm, fun-loving and impulsive. She really is a very pleasant person to be with and can be the life of a party. The difficulty begins to surface when you ask for a commitment. Let's suppose we ask her to dinner along with some of our other friends. She is always the first to promise to be there. Absolutely sure. However, when the time comes around for the visit, she just dosn't show. No apology, no excuse, no rationale, just no show! This happens over and over again. Gradually we learn that it is a difficulty we just have to live with.

In the business environment, the extreme friendly person gives vague instructions and is apologetic when delegating. An instruction may go something like this: "Susan, I really hate bothering you. I know how busy you are and I hate giving you more work to add to the heavy load you already have. However, the truth is I don't want to trust this important job to anyone else. I hope you don't mind me asking you to do this little task."

Average "dominant" behaviour was described in Chapter 4 as task-oriented. These people are pre-occupied with getting things done. They are the movers and shakers, in that they are always concerned about delivery. Because of their preoccupation with results, they sometimes overlook the feelings and emotions of real people. They might even look at people as instruments to help them in their efforts to obtain results. In some instances, they might forget that people are human beings like themselves.

Again, difficult behaviour in this quadrant is these behavioural traits taken to an extreme degree. Extremely dominant people argue and dictate. They put pressure on people to achieve their objectives. They fight. They are belligerent. They are arrogant, brash and pushy. They like telling people what to do. The best example of a "difficult dominant" I can think of is Jim. People stay away from Jim if they can help it. When the news is announced that Jim is coming for a visit, the spontaneous response is, "Oh no! not again." Jim, you see, makes it difficult for people around him. He finds fault with everything, and then tells you the right way to do it. "That colour isn't right for your living room. You should have chosen a brighter blue. Next time try to match things better." He has an opinion about everything, and a solution for all your problems.

In the business environment the extreme dominant person gives orders more like a captain in the army. Instructions are curt and abrasive: "Susan, this is to be done by tomorrow at noon. Try to do it right this time."

The average "cautious" person is a combination of "serious" and "listener." This person is the observing type. He is cautious in his approach to decisions and tends to want as much information as is possible to get. While this is a desirable characteristic, he tends to take it beyond a realistic point; and it results in frustration for others.

The difficult people in this quadrant take these behavioural traits to an extreme degree. They tend to be overly cautious and look for opportunities to delay decisions. Sometimes excuses for delays result in picky and suspicious behaviour. They quite often appear to be uninvolved, withdrawn and sullen.

A good example of a difficult "cautious" is David. David doesn't talk much and spends a lot of time by himself. He is capable and academically-able, but will often give the impression of not knowing much. His standard answer to questions that involve his opinions or knowledge is, "I don't know." David seems to always want to be sure before he does anything. He is quite often frustratingly quiet and indecisive. In the work environment, David is cautious and suspicious. He is reluctant to give others any level of autonomy. He is a poor delegator tending not to trust anybody. A favourite saying of his is, "If you want something done right, you've got to do it yourself." When giving instructions, it usually is flavoured with doubt and apprehension as in: "Susan I want you to be very careful with this job. There is a potential for all kinds of problems to develop. Please read over the instructions very carefully and advise me if you have any questions. Do you think you can get it done by tomorrow?"

The "expressive" person brings a lot of sunshine and song. She is a sales person. Not necessarily with regard to her career, but certainly as it relates to her style. These people are a combination of "warm" and "talkative" and find it easy to express themselves in a positive way.

Difficult people in this quadrant take sunshine and song to an extreme degree though. They weary you with the intensity of their positive nature and happy-go-lucky style. They exert great bursts of energy, followed by equally great bursts of depression. Their emotional swings from positive to negative and vice versa is sometimes unnerving. Their impulsive nature sometimes develops into hyperactive behaviour.

Jackie is a good example of this. She talks incessantly and wearies her friends with her high energy level and enthusiasm. When told that she talks a lot, she responds with, "Everybody knows I talk a lot." The implication is that she came out of the talkative mould at birth, and there is not much she can do about it. As far as she is concerned, the matter ends there.

Extreme "expressive" people tend to exaggerate their own achievements as well as the achievements of others. They tend to dramatize a lot, and this quite often comes out when they give instructions, as in: "Susan you shouldn't have any problem with this task. After all I did it correctly on my first try. I know you will do a good job. I am sure you will have it finished by tomorrow at noon."

We have compared average behaviour with difficult behaviour in the four basic styles of human behaviour. Difficult behaviour is merely average behaviour taken to an extreme. It's as if someone got an over supply of "friendly" behaviour at birth, or another had the gift of an overly "expressive" nature. This "excess" behaviour builds tension in us because of the differences that are so obvious. The final factor that identifies a person as a difficult person is the factor of inflexibility.

■ *Meet inflexibility with compromise*

Don't expect to get understanding from difficult people. One of the things they lack is the ability to see the other side of the coin. If there is one consistent quality about difficult people, it is their capacity to see only their side of the story. Their inflexibility is frustrating. Even when "the other cheek is turned," they will persist in being adamant and demanding. Compromise is not part of their world.

Just recently a concerned participant in a workshop asked the following question: "What would you do if your boss told you your style is too lenient, and you need to act in a stronger and more aggressive way. But you feel good about yourself and don't want to change the way you are now?" My answer to him was: "Maybe the first thing you want to do is listen, and then listen again! Maybe your boss has a point, and he sees something you don't see. Further, it may not be necessary to change your style but learn the need for flexibility. There are times when it is quite acceptable to be friendly, caring and supportive, and then there are other times when you need to be more dominant in your style. There are situations that demand a stronger more assertive response. Your judgement should tell you when this is necessary, and you should be flexible enough to be able to change and respond appropriately to the situation."

■ *Socialize appropriately*

For "extreme friendly" people, try socializing appropriately. Extreme friendly behaviour results from
some basic personal needs. The world of the
extremely friendly person is filled with concerns and
preoccupations about social acceptance and popu-
larity. Their behaviour is prompted by a deep need
for friendship and social acceptance. Their internal
dialogue is an ongoing discussion of "I wonder if she
likes me?" or "What can I do to make him my
friend?" This person is concerned with his acceptance
among colleagues and acquaintances. He is constantly
preoccupied with the kind of behaviour that will
attract favourable attention. He wants to make an
impression that will result in a high level of acceptance. He wants to be popular.

Raymond was a good example of that kind of behaviour. Raymond was a school chum going back to
college days. He stands out still in my mind as a
difficult person. He would approach a group of boys
with a wide, artificial smile, throw his arm around
the shoulders of the nearest person and in a loud,
insincere voice remark, "Real good to see you all."
Everything about Raymond's actions had a flavour of
artificiality. We quickly recognized that Raymond's
friendliness was motivated by his own personal, unreasonable needs. He seemed to want the approval,
recognition and adoration of everyone he met. He
seemed obsessed with being everybody's friend.

The result was to achieve the very opposite. Nobody wanted him around. He made us uncomfortable with his obvious, insincere advances and his artificial friendliness. What do you do with a Raymond?

Treat overly-friendly people with normal, realistic behaviour. Don't respond in kind with artificial behaviour. Socialize appropriately, by treating them as a natural, normal human being. Accept them as a person, while ignoring their unrealistic and abnormal friendly behaviour. Send them the subtle message that their insincerity is not appreciated. Show them you are willing to be human and sensitive, but you are not willing to indulge in insincere or artificial behaviour.

In the business environment, be careful to be impartial with overly-friendly individuals. Employees and co-workers will sometimes act in overly-friendly ways to try to secure favours from their managers. They might give gifts or do favours to try to get an inside track with them.

Perhaps you have a Susan in your office. Susan would quite often enter her manager's office to have a "confidential" chat. This would involve a tale or two of the latest comments from some of Susan's co-workers. For instance: "Jane said this company doesn't care much about us. She said she feels like looking for another job." Susan is trying to get an inside track with her boss through building a special relationship. You want to be careful to let Susan know you do not appreciate "office gossip." You respect her as a person, but you will not be manipulated by her into a special relationship or friendship.

Overly-friendly people have to be treated firmly and sometimes formally. In time they will get the message their artificial and insincere behaviour is recognized, and they cannot make any headway with you. Be consistent, firm and impartial.

■ *Be assertive, not aggressive*

Be assertive, but not aggressive with an "extreme dominant" person. The world of the extremely-dominant person is filled with scenes of confrontations, conflicts and wars. She is constantly asserting herself. She never seems to want to be found making a mistake. Her opinion must be always right. She is arrogant.

This attitude flows out of a need for high, personal esteem and independence. The internal dialogue has an emphasis on, "I am the greatest."

A recent article in our local paper suggests that of the four behavioural styles, employees complain most about a "dominant" boss. The author describes this type of difficult person as preferrring talking to listening and demanding rather than questioning. He is often quite moody. This type of boss is also quick to argue, dictate and make arbitrary decisions. How do we deal with this kind of difficult person?

The biggest mistake is to act subserviently and allow an "extreme dominant" to roll right over you. Stand up and be heard. Be assertive, but not aggressive. Years ago I worked for a classic "extreme dominant." On one memorable occasion, I sat in his office for over an hour as he ranted and raved about the inefficiency of suppliers, and one in particular with whom he had a problem. He ordered me to write an aggressive letter, demanding a refund for expenses caused through late delivery from this supplier. The supplier happened to be one of the largest corporations in the country.

After he had exhausted his anger and his energy, I calmly and assertively suggested that the letter he was instructing me to write was not, in my opinion, a good idea. I said it would create further hostility with our supplier, which might eventually result in a termination of the relationship. He listened but insisted I write the letter. The response from the supplier was a sharply-worded reply, expressing disdain for his request. He subsequently avoided any discussion of the matter, but I sensed a raised level of respect for my opinions during subsequent conversations.

Complying weakly and submissively to the demands of dominant people is nearly always counterproductive. A sad and tragic example of this was Neville Chamberlain's response to the aggressive, arrogant Hitler in 1938. A more assertive response to Hitler's demands may have changed the course of history.

Understand the world of the "extreme dominant." They see themselves as strong and knowledgeable. They tend to respect those who are like them. So show an assertive and strong response to the behaviour of this type of difficult person. Be careful though to recognize their independence and authority. Remember, they think very highly of themselves and are not about to let others challenge that self-image without a spirited response.

■ *Exercise patience*

What would it be like to live in the world of the extremely-cautious person? Well, for starters, here is the kind of dialogue you would hear constantly: "I don't trust anybody." "What proof do you have for that?" "Let me think about it for a little, and I'll get back to you." Cautious people frustrate us because they seem to carry the mandate to "be careful" beyond reasonable limits. They see gremlins and monsters where the average person sees a tame dog. They imagine storm warnings when most of us see only blue skies and sunshine. They are pessimistic, distrustful and passive. They are "no" people in the sense that they are always looking for reasons why it can't be done. They will sometimes work against something just to prove that it's not a good idea to be too optimistic.

How do we deal with the "extreme cautious" person? We exercise patience with them. We acknowledge that their concerns are legitimate. Then show them that although possible, in most instances, the scenario they fear is highly improbable. Bring statistics to show them their scenario is not likely· to be realized. Show them some risk is involved in everything we do. Even in bed we can be smothered by a pillow or inadvertently roll off and break our necks. However, experience shows this rarely happens, so it is reasonably safe to go to bed and have a good night's rest. Try not to ridicule their stances though, as they can just as quickly cite instances where their fears actually took place.

■ *Acknowledge their achievements*

Jennifer is an "extreme expressive." She feels good about herself and considers herself an achiever. She usually enters a room expressing high energy through body language and voice. Her posture is confident and strong and her voice is loud. She shatters the silence!

Jennifer brings a lot of sunshine with her. Trouble is a little sunshine is good, but too much can end in a serious case of sunburn and subsequent illness. Jennifer is carrying the elements of warmth and impulsiveness to an inappropriate level. We become uncomfortable with the intensity of her personality and begin to withdraw. Jennifer's objective of making a great impression is counterproductive, since instead of drawing us she is driving us. What can we do for Jennifer?

For starters, we can try to neutralize the intensity of her personality and lower the level of warmth so that it becomes more bearable. How? By setting a slower pace. "Relax Jennifer," we might say. Let her begin to realize her pace is too fast, too intense, too uncomfortable for us. We can also slow our rate of speech in response to the overly-animated and fast pace Jennifer is using. We can reduce the intensity of our gestures and adopt a quieter voice. This will have the effect of slowing Jennifer down to a comfortable and more acceptable level.

In a business environment an "extreme expressive" is confident and articulate. He is an achiever and he can't really understand why other people have not achieved what he has. This makes him a little impatient with people. That's exactly the way Albert is. Albert is a wonderful speaker and a great role model on the platform.

However, when Albert has to deal with people on a personal basis he runs into problems. He is arrogant, confrontational and emotional. He is adamant in his views and tends to speak out without considering the long term effects. As a result, he gets a lot of people upset. He gets them working against him. His intentions are good, but his methods are counter-productive. He is sometimes shocked that others are not aware of his good intentions and can't overlook his constant bursts of impatience. If we could look inside Albert's head, we would see this kind of dialogue going on: "After all I only want the best for everyone, so what's the big fuss about a little indiscretion. People are too thin-skinned anyway. Why can't you folks act like adults and grow up."

The way to deal with Albert is to acknowledge his achievements. Let him know he has excelled in his chosen career. Appeal to his desire for further personal achievement by showing him how his inappropriate behaviour is destroying his image. Show him that persisting in extreme expressive behaviour will eventually hurt and possibly destroy his successful career.

■ *Put on your raincoat*

A few nights ago I listened to a radio talk show on dealing with difficult people. One of the callers described a situation where her mother had succeeded in frustrating the entire family. Every day the family awoke to a diatribe of criticisms, complaints and accusations. The caller, a young girl, said it had come to the point where she herself had been forced to leave the house. But now she was concerned about her two brothers left at home. They were under the power of her mother and were expressing frustration, disgust and disrespect. In desperate tones, the caller asked what could be done about this situation.

"Don't let it get to you," was the firm response from the radio station. "Don't allow any of that negative sludge to be internalized. Keep it on the outside where it belongs." The consultant then went on to explain that one of the worst things you can do when dealing with difficult people is to act from a position of fear, anger or resentment. "Don't allow the actions of difficult people to arouse anger and resentment in you," he insisted. "Keep your emotional balance, protect your self esteem and maintain your composure."

When dealing with a difficult person you must protect your emotional control and make sure that none of the criticisms, accusations or undesirable behaviour get inside and begin to cause emotional upset. You must learn how to protect your fragile emotional balance by building a protective wall that effectively neutralizes the verbal attack of the difficult person.

One way to do this is by imaginatively putting on a protective garment. For instance, you might mentally put on a hypothetical raincoat, and imagine the barbs and darts coming your way are rain drops. The raincoat is your protection to hold the barbs at bay. Use any scenario you wish, as long as you successfully prevent the accusations and criticisms from gaining entry to your emotional state. Ways and strategies for maintaining and enhancing self-worth and personal confidence are the subject of Chapter 9.

In the first workshops I conducted years ago, if anyone challenged or contradicted any of the statements I made, I tended to regard that person as difficult. Their criticism cut me deeply, and I would quickly try to justify my stand. I interpreted their contribution as an attack, and because my confidence level was low I became defensive and doubtful. Today when I am challenged or confronted on a perspective or outlook, I rather welcome that development. No more does it affect my confidence level. I do not allow it to affect my emotional state. I accept it for what it is, another perspective to be appreciated, examined and analysed. Actually, I am happy to hear disagreement as it causes me to examine my own beliefs and convictions more closely, as well as prompting a lively and constructive discussion.

"Putting on your raincoat" will help you to act in a more responsible and mature way. The control you express will tend to have a calming and quietening effect on the difficult person. This could result in that person becoming more reasonable and receptive with a potential for a satisfactory agreement.

■ *Build a reserve account*

When dealing with difficult people you need to build a reserve account with them.

If you were dealing with a bank, you would hardly try drawing cheques on your account if you had not previously deposited some money. Making deposits at the right time, enables you to draw cheques when you need to. If we deal with difficult people and try to "draw cheques" before we make deposits, we will have a problem. As we try to get cooperation from them with an empty account we will find we have nothing to draw on.

Look for opportunities to make deposits with the difficult people you come in contact with. Deposits such as "Thank you" at appropriate times, positive reinforcement for a job well done, or time spent listening to their agendas. Show them the respect that is due them as a part of the human race. You may not like their behaviour, but you cannot deny them membership in our society. Giving a little gift, or some gesture that says you are thinking of them in a positive way might be in order. If you have a positive "bank balance" with a difficult person, you stand a good chance of getting cooperation and ultimate agreement with them.

Pause and think of the most difficult person you have to deal with. Could you make a list of the things about this person that frustrate and upset you? "That's easy," you say. Now, could you make a list of the things about this person that are positive, desirable and commendable? Regardless of what you said, this person has some positive, admirable qualities. Take the time to start a list and continue to add to it as you think of new positive things about that person. Use this list to make some deposits in your reserve account. The more you have in the account, the better chance you have of improving the relationship with that person.

■ *Reverse roles*

When none of the above seems to work try reversing roles. That means exchanging places with the difficult person. It means persuading the difficult person to "walk in your shoes" or put themselves in your place. It means forcing them to be a little more empathetic. When you say to a difficult person, "What would you do if you were in my place?" It obligates them to begin to think a little more about how they would respond to their own behaviour.

I had an experience with a colleague that illustrates the power of reversing roles. Earl had been opposing some policies in an organization we both belonged to and was generally making a real nuisance of himself. It was my responsibility to implement these new policies, which most of our associates felt were for the good of our organization. All except Earl. He was adamant that they should be abandoned or changed drastically. During a confrontation one day, I challenged Earl with the question, "What would you do if you were in my place?" For a moment he seemed taken aback by the question. Then I saw the wheels begin to turn in his mind. I saw him putting himself in my place and in the place of his fellow associates, and I saw a certain amount of understanding begin to develop. His tone of voice became less strident, his manner became more positive and he allowed that perhaps there were some aspects of the policies that were helpful. His opposition to the policies became less intense and gradually abated entirely.

Sometimes reversing roles can get you home from far away places. During a vacation in Jamaica, I had to deal with a problem with our return ticket that had the potential of causing us to miss our flight. The airline representative I was dealing with was being most difficult. She was aloof and formal. She was treating me like just another statistic that had a problem. I could sense her thinking: "So what if you have to miss your flight. Sometimes people have to miss flights. Why should you be any different?" I realized that somehow I had to break through the cold, hard wall that seemed to exist between us. Somehow I had to reach the emotions of this lady and build a relationship. So I waited for the appropriate moment and then said: "Gloria, you have a lot of experience in getting people to different places. You probably know the solution to the kind of problem I am faced with now. Tell me, what would you do if you found yourself in the situation I find myself in now?" It worked like a charm. Her first response was to laugh. The wall fell down! She then criticised me a little for not anticipating this kind of problem, and then went on to suggest what I might do. The good news is we got home and on time. Chalk up another victory for reversing roles.

■ *Check on yourself*

Are you sure *YOU* are not the problem? You see, you might be the difficult person without even knowing it. So inadvertently, you are constantly creating climates and shaping situations which encourage tension. If the chemistry between two people is wrong, the result will be conflict. You may be contributing to that chemistry without even knowing it. So checking on yourself could be a revelation.

An anecdote I love to tell in workshops concerns little Johnny who was about ten years old. According to how I heard the story, Johnny asked Mr. Johnston if he could use his telephone. Mr. Johnston was the owner of the pharmacy in the little town where Johnny lived. Reluctantly, Mr Johnston gave permission. "Please be short, Johnny. I have customers that may be wanting to get in to order prescriptions," he warned. "Not to worry" said Johnny, "I'll just be a minute."

Johnny dials his number, and waits for an answer. Mr. Johnston can't help but hear the following conversation: "Hello, is that Mr. Black? Mr. Black, I'm

a little boy about ten years old and I would very
much like to get a job in your store." (short pause)
"I see...you already have a little boy. But Mr. Black
I'm a very enthusiastic little boy and I really like to
work, and I am sure you would like me." (another
short pause) "I see....your little boy is very enthusiastic too and he really likes to work and you like
him. I understand Mr. Black, but I am willing to
work for very reasonable wages, and I just know I
would do a good job." (long pause) "I see....you are
very happy with your little boy's wages and his
work. Well, thank you for your time Mr. Black, and
I am sorry to have bothered you. Good bye."

The moment Johnny gets off the phone he starts to
dance and sing with delight. He is so happy that
Mr. Johnston looks on bewildered. "What's with you
Johnny? You didn't get the job," says Mr. Johnston.
"The job?" says Johnny. "The job? I already have
the job. I'm just checking on myself."

It's great when you check on yourself and you get
the kind of answer Johnny got. But what if after
checking you find others see you as a troublemaker
and a nuisance. What if you find out you are the
cause of the problems in the department, instead of
Mary who you have been accusing all along? Now
it requires a brave and confident person to acknowledge that *you* are the difficult person. Not
only that, but courage to begin to do something
about it.

I have a letter in my files written about twenty
years ago by an employee who was my assistant at
that time. I asked her to write it. When Carmen

was leaving, I asked her if she would do me a favour and tell me in a letter what she thought of my management skills. At first she thought I was joking, but when I insisted, she agreed to comply. In that letter she gave me some accolades, but she also pointed out a few areas in which my management skills could improve greatly. Through the years I have tried to address the things she pointed out.

Honest feedback from peers is a necessary factor in trying to find out the kind of image we are communicating to others. Sometimes the last person to know we are getting on other people's nerves is ourselves. There is not much you can do about your own difficult behaviour, if you don't even know about it. So don't be afraid to ask for the feedback that is crucial to your growth as an effective employee, manager or good friend. Checking on yourself is a positive activity.

■ *Confront negative behaviour*

The best way to explain confronting is to tell you exactly how I learned about it. A group of managers were discussing difficult people and I happened to be facilitating the discussion. I'll never forget what Ron told us. He said in his company there was a tendency to avoid dealing with a difficult person. Managers would sometimes resort to transferring the difficult person, or at other times just turning a blind eye to the whole affair. Of course that resulted in greater problems, since - in the case of a transfer - the difficult person transferred his negative behaviour to another arena. In the case of an avoidance of the issue, co-workers became upset because nothing was done to correct the unacceptable behaviour.

Ron then went on to describe how to confront. When we confront a difficult person we make the person understand the matter is serious and we intend to deal with it in a forthright way. We might say for instance, "John, I would like to see you in my office at 9:00 a.m. tomorrow. At that meeting, I intend to make you aware of our expectations for your job, and we will discuss how you are measuring up against those expectations. Consider this to be a formal meeting, so you might like to be prepared for it." This is the first step towards confronting.

At the meeting your first concern should be to help John acknowledge or agree there is a problem. This usually is the biggest challenge of all. If you can get by this step successfully, you might find the rest fairly easy. Most difficult people don't see the problem. They wonder out loud what all the fuss is about. They rationalize, explain and give excuses. They dodge the issues and fudge the facts. Your challenge is to have the kind of evidence that will persuade John there is indeed a problem.

If you can get past this hurdle, the next step is to involve John in finding a solution for the problem. Ask him directly. "John, now that we have agreed there is an unacceptable situation is there anything you can do to correct it?" You just might be surprised to hear John making a suggestion that is acceptable to you. If and when this happens, John's commitment to the solution will be strong. After all it was his solution, and he is very likely to take ownership of the action he suggested. The ideal outcome would be that his behaviour improves and everybody lives happily ever after.

Of course, none of us are naive enough to think this will always happen, but the specific steps on how to confront will help us to handle the situation with confidence and aplomb. One last step - Ron told us to remember - was to always give positive reinforcement when behaviour improves. So the steps in sequence for confronting are: get agreement that there is a problem, involve the person in solving the problem, agree on a solution, positively reinforce improved behaviour.

Find the common ground

Difficult people focus on the differences in a conflict. For them the interpersonal landscape becomes a forest of weeds and thorns and they miss the flowers present. They get so preoccupied with the negatives they forget there are positives present. If we can shift their perspective and help them to become aware of the common ground, we can begin to build a foundation for agreement and subsequent change of behaviour.

How do we do that? We ask questions that open up the difficult person and allow the specific issues to surface. Mutual goals and objectives begin to appear.

Hidden under the exterior of difficult behaviour there is sometimes a productive employee seeking release.   It takes patience, empathy and caring to bring out the best in them.   Finding the common ground can act as a foundation for a dialogue that will lead towards rapport and agreement.

12 ways with Difficult People

- Enter their world

- Identify their style

- Meet inflexibility with compromise

- Socialize appropriately

- Be assertive, not aggressive

- Exercise patience

- Acknowledge their achievements

- Put on your raincoat

- Build a reserve account

- Reverse roles

- Check on yourself

- Confront negative behaviour

Chapter 7

21 STRATEGIES FOR SUCCESSFUL EVERYDAY NEGOTIATION

Keep your eye on the real objective

Remember Pearl Graham that we talked about in Chapter 4? She was that delightful person who comes into a room and looks around and says, "Gee, you all look so good."

Pearl had an experience that is a good example of long-term thinking, and the advantages of investing a little now to earn a lot later. Pearl called me up one day and described the following situation. She had made a commitment to a car dealer some weeks before that she would buy a certain car. The dealer promised that the car with extras would be delivered on a certain day. To bind the deal she deposited $500 with the dealer. However, after some discussion and many phone calls, the sales manager for the dealer advised her that delivery of the car had to be extended. Not only that, but the colour she had ordered was not available.

The attitude and manner of the sales manager was so casual that Pearl decided she would cancel her order with the dealer and request her deposit be returned. When she advised the sales manager of her decision, she was rather surprised and a little angry at his response. He insisted that he could not refund her the $500 deposit.

It was at this point Pearl contacted me and asked for my advice. I thought about it a little and concluded that the owner of the dealership had to be a forward-looking and sensible business person.   So I encouraged Pearl to ask for a meeting with the general manager and explain the circumstances to him. "Be courteous and calm," I said. "Tell him that you have a high regard for the dealership. Tell him that you are quite surprised that his company would try to take advantage of a client, especially when they were not able to deliver what they had promised." I suggested that she not be demanding but present her case in a reasonable manner.

The result of course, was just as I expected. The general manager, faced with a pleasant but assertive young lady, saw the short-term implications. $500 in the company's bank account would be nice to have, but it would also upset and anger Pearl to the point that she might take legal action or report the matter to the appropriate customer service department with local government. He could do without that kind of negative publicity. He could also do without Pearl telling everyone within range the absolutely insensitive treatment that she had from the dealership. The long-term advantage would be to get Pearl on the side of the dealership and win her back for another sale. Even if this did not occur, at least she would speak positively of the dealership to her friends and acquaintances.

This sounds like heresy

Human nature seems to prompt us to act in ways that satisfy short-term needs. It's so easy to see just what will benefit us today and not see the implications over the long term. Good negotiators always keep their eyes on the long-term result.

I remember once having a conversation with a manager who was involved with some union/management negotiations. He was telling me that during the negotiation sessions that year, management had reached all the goals they had set for themselves. In other words, management had won! He was sharing with me that the time had now come for the union to win. There was a definite plan to allow the union to win a few rounds. The negotiations were being approached with a strategic plan to give in to some of the union demands.

This sounded like heresy from a management negotiator. And yet, this executive realized that if the management side continued to "win" all the areas of disagreement, it would not be long before the union members would become so frustrated and upset that the working relationship would suffer significantly. So a firm decision was made to allow some concessions at the next round of negotiations. A good example of long-term thinking.

Strong, trusting, productive relationships

Most of our everyday negotiations are long term. For instance, we are constantly negotiating with the people we work with. We try to work out disagreements and problems with our co-workers, bosses or employees. The same can be said of those at home. Our spouses quite often disagree with our way of looking at things. Our children disagree with our decisions relating to their life styles and ideas. All this presents situations that have to be addressed and worked out.

Short-term strategies are short sighted. We need to look at the events and circumstances with a focus on, "How will this affect my relationship with this person next week, next month, next year? Will my decision threaten the good relationship that has existed up until now? Am I determined to satisfy this need now, knowing that it will jeopardize my relationship with this person for a long time to come?" A long-term perspective builds strong, trusting, productive relationships. Quite often the last laugh goes to the person that looked at the problem and its long-term implications.

Honesty is number One

"Can I trust him?" Marcus was saying to me. "How do I know that he won't take advantage of me and take me for all I am worth?" Marcus was talking about a friend of mine. I had recommended that he contact my friend because of a certain need that existed. Marcus had made the contact and a problem had arisen. My friend had failed to communicate clearly and Marcus was worried. The inevitable barrier of mistrust was building up. "Can I trust him?" he asked again.

I felt comfortable in telling Marcus that if my friend followed the pattern of behaviour that he had followed over the past four years, he had nothing to worry about. My friend had shown high-ethical behaviour with clear expressions of honesty and respect. In all our transactions and relationships he had shown fairness and a sensitivity for my opinions and perspectives. We had not always agreed on the details of plans that we formulated, but these disagreements were handled with such respect and courtesy that the relationship continued to be a cordial one. I told Marcus that I had the highest respect and trust in my friend's integrity. I said that I was sure that their negotiations would prove to be cordial and satisfying over the long term. If we all could have that kind of confidence in those we have to negotiate with, we would be assured that most, if not all of our everyday negotiations, would come out to win-win outcomes.

The result is what you promised

Being honest is merely being dependable. A nice definition of honesty surfaced in a seminar some years ago. The participant said, "Honesty is when

the result is what you promised." What you said
would happen did happen. After a while people
begin to notice that what you say you really mean.
They can depend on you. When this happens, people
begin to want to deal with you because they know
where they are with you. They don't have to guess
or worry about the result. The result is what you
promised.

That quality, although desirable, is not found too
often. Our world has too high a proportion of
people who make promises they can't fulfil. Sometimes promises are given for the purpose of manipulating others. Nowhere is this seen as much as in
the field of politics. The image of politicians has
never been lower and more in disrespect than it is
today. The unethical few continue to make promises
they never expect to fulfil. They prey on the gullible.
They make promises to them right up until voting
time. And then as soon as the mark has been made
and the votes counted, they forget they ever said
that. When questioned, the newly elected tell long
stories about past administration errors, pressures
from special interest groups and the environment. All
this may be true. But it was common knowledge
long before they took office. They promised, knowing
they would never be able to deliver.

Dishonesty rampant in business

Unethical behaviour in business is commonplace. The
public almost expects it now. For instance, in situations where tax deductions have been made and the
resulting decrease passed on to the consumer, most

consumers know and accept that the promised deduction will never get to the retail level. Somewhere along the way the deduction will be added to company profits to increase the business bottom line. The public expects that. But along with that expectation goes a deep distrust of all activities of business. The result is a lack of loyalty. People look for the best buy with a harsh disregard for loyalty where an organization is concerned.

Some good news

But there is some good news! For years I have been loyal to my corner service station. I buy my gas there, I get my car repaired there, I buy my tires there and I even bought a car from Gerry. Why? Because when Gerry says he is going to do something he delivers. Gerry tells me sometimes that I can get something done to my car at a lower cost elsewhere. I tell him that I appreciate him being honest with me, but I would like him to go ahead with the repair anyway. You see, I know it will be fixed the right way when Gerry does it. If it is not, I can take it back to him and know that I won't get the endless run around and hassle that I might get somewhere else. Gerry is reliable. He has business ethics and his word is his bond. We hardly ever write anything on paper. Gerry just tells me what the price will be and what he will do. That's not good business practice, but when you find someone you can trust you take those kinds of chances. I wish we had more people like Gerry in the business world.

■ *Learn to read people*

When you meet someone for the first time, there is a lot at stake. They are going to form opinions of you and you are going to form opinions of them. The meeting could be the start of a fulfilling relationship and a satisfying friendship. On the other hand, it could be the beginning of tension and dislike. A lot depends on what happens in those first few moments as you stand eyeball to eyeball with outstretched hands greeting each other.

One of the things you may want to keep in mind is that this person is going to be different from you. What kind of person is this anyway? Is he a friendly, sensitive and caring person who will want to give some thought to my needs and ambitions? Or, on the other hand, is he a belligerent and proud person who thinks of himself only and wants to bulldoze his way through life. If you can recognize the style of the person before you, you can appropriately respond and begin to build a positive relationship.

I met Jack Richardson last month and it wasn't long before the real Jack began to show through. In the initial greeting he was every bit the poised and thoughtful manager. Then within minutes, I began to perceive that Jack was an arrogant, overbearing and insensitive boss. His remarks told me that he felt those reporting to him were nothing more than "production units" to be manipulated as he saw fit. He knew what was best for them, and he was instructing me to give them the medicine that he knew was best for them. "I am going to rough them up a bit, so I want you to come in and pour some oil on the rough water." Now that I knew who I was dealing with it gave me a better chance to negotiate with him. I responded to Jack's curt, focused approach by being short and focused myself. He was businesslike, so I was businesslike too. He was alert, serious and to the point, and I matched his style accordingly.

How to build rapport

Matching the style of another person is called "matching and pacing." It is a strategy that helps to build rapport in the early moments of a meeting. When someone meets you he is unconsciously looking for the things he likes in you. Usually the things he likes in you are the things he likes in himself. In other words, people like to see in you the things they are exhibiting when they meet you.

If they are exhibiting businesslike and professional behaviour, they want to see that in you also. A similar response from you makes them feel more comfortable with you. If, on the other hand, the person you are meeting is exhibiting a friendly, open and gushing approach that is the behaviour he would like to see in you. If this is not forthcoming, it tends to build tension. The person will feel that you are not responding in an appropriate manner and will assume you do not appreciate his visit.

Tension will begin to build and depending on the change or lack of change that takes place, the meeting will drift into frustration and impasse.

Match and pace for positive results

I remember watching a situation develop that started off with all the ingredients for success but ended in failure because the persons involved failed to "match and pace." I was asked to attend a meeting where training in a large organization was being planned. Three of us were to be in attendance: Jeff, a consultant in the business of training, Harry the training supervisor with the company and me.

I had met Harry before and had found him to be a breath of fresh air. He was relaxed, humorous and easy to talk to. I was amused as I watched Jeff and him meet for the first time. Jeff was a businesslike, serious type of person. Initially, Harry made a few humorous remarks, but Jeff was unresponsive. Jeff seemed impatient to get on with the matter we had come to discuss, while Harry seemed in no hurry to get to the point.

Jeff, of course, was at a disadvantage since he did not know Harry as well as I did. I knew that Harry after some initial small talk would get into the subject and be very direct and professional. However the bad start to this meeting developed into a visible dislike between Jeff and Harry. As the meeting continued we became involved in a tour of the facilities. By the time we got to the end of the tour, these two were hardly talking to each other. I was a little amused at the developments, as I had anticipated this result when I saw the early responses of both parties. The need for an effort to build the right kind of climate is profoundly important. If the right setting is not reached, then negative developments are bound to take place. If, on the other hand, care is taken to build the right kind of positive climate, good things will nearly always happen.

■ *Take control*

Gerard Nierenberg is considered to be one of the leading authorities on negotiation in North America. Nierenberg has written many books and leads seminars on effective negotiation. Some sage advice Nierenberg dispenses is: "Preparation makes an amateur look like a professional."

If you want to come out of your negotiations with more win-win outcomes, you must take time to prepare appropriately. Just a few minutes gathering your thoughts and preparing a suitable strategy might make the difference between a happy ending or an experience in frustration. Preparation will help you feel more comfortable in your everyday exchanges and will position you to negotiate and capture your share of the pie. It will put you in control.

When were you last at an auction sale? My last one taught me a very important lesson about being prepared for a negotiation. At the time I worked for a heavy equipment leasing organization. Our

National Sales Manager Ron and I attended on this occasion. As we entered the warehouse where the equipment was, we noticed a welding machine that had evidently just been repaired and painted. It really looked good. Ron asked me what we were paying for this machine from the factory currently. "$2000, Ron," I said. "What do you think we should pay for it today?" he asked. This got me thinking.

The machine looked like it was in mint condition, but of course we had no idea what might be wrong inside. We really had to take a risk, since the equipment had to be bought without any warranty or return options. We discussed the matter of possible internal problems, the condition of the machine, the possibility of repair work as well as the chance that the machine might be just as good as it looked. Finally, we decided that $1000 was as far as we would go, all things considered. I remember Ron saying, "O.K., we'll bid with others up to $1000, but as soon as the bidding gets to that level we will withdraw. In effect, we will walk away. It will not be in our interest to negotiate further. We will have reached our maximum, and we will stop negotiating." That was the most important decision we made that day. We had decided on our "walk away point" and now we were prepared for the negotiation.

■ *Find your walk-away point*

Whether you are going to an auction sale or a union/management negotiation; whether you are negotiating with your spouse about a new family car or with your boss about a raise, you need to know exactly when you have reached your maximum. You must understand very clearly, what you want from the negotiation. You must know the extent to which you will go, or the price you are willing to pay; and you must know this before you start the negotiation.

You may wonder why it's so important to know your "walk away point" before you go into the negotiation. The answer is simple. Once you are in a negotiation or discussion, emotions start to invade you and affect your decisions. The job of an auctioneer or indeed any negotiator is to influence you through pressure, threats, benefits, incentives or charisma. Without some preparation for this kind of onslaught you will be open to the many ways people have of manipulating you. But if you have a point which you will not go beyond, it becomes very helpful in making a decision. Walk-away points provide psychological power because they help you to know where you are in a situation.

Not thinking the situation through and deciding where and when it is in your best interest to forego further negotiation is naive. A good auctioneer can work wonders in a crowd where no one has prepared a point to stop at. The auctioneer keeps working on the emotions. "If you just move it up a little more the object of your affection can be yours." You keep moving the number up and before you know it you have paid more for that item than you would have paid in a store. And at the store you would have had a warranty!

■ *Protect your territory*

So the first law of preparation is to know where you want to go, and decide on a specific number or place or principle, which will be your place to stop. Once that has been identified, you will want to take every precaution that no one knows where that place is. That is your secret weapon. When the other side has no idea where you will stop in the negotiation, you can ask for anything you want. They will have no idea where you are, or how much you are willing to lower your demands or indeed if you will lower them at all. However, if they do get wind of the point at which you will walk away, they can very carefully move you closer to that point before they conclude the negotiation.

Let's go back to our auction sale to make that point clear. If Ron and I had revealed to the auctioneer that day that we were willing to pay $1000 for the machine, what do you suppose the auctioneer might have done? He would have had a number of options open to him. First, he might have put somebody in the sale to boost the price and make sure that it did go to $1000. Another option he had was to accept a cheque from us before the sale and not put the unit on auction at all. His rationale might have been, "I have no idea what this machine will sell for. Here is an opportunity to get $1000 for it. Perhaps I would be wise to take it while I have it." Of course we will never know, since we did not tell him. What we do know however, is that when the machine went on auction, the bidding only got to $300. We walked away with a deal because we successfully concealed our "walk-away point." The same thing can happen to you if you carefully conceal the walk-away point that you decide on in your negotiations.

Do I really need it?

One of the questions that you need to ask yourself as you prepare for a negotiation should be, "Is this a need or a want?" Is this something that you absolutely must have, or is this just something that it would be nice to have? Remember that your walk-away point is the last and final point before you stop negotiating. Beyond this point you are going to be worse off than you were before. Not only are your "wants" not being considered, but your absolute needs are being bartered away at this point. You would be foolish to do this.

As you prepare for a decision on your walk-away point, you might like to ask yourself some very focused questions: "If I cannot get agreement on my needs, what will I do?" "Do I have an alternative?" "Who has the power in this negotiation and will they use it indiscriminately?" "What is the last and final point before I would give in? What would happen after if I did give in?" This sort of focused analysis will help you see the consequences of being too stubborn and what the price of that might be. It might encourage you to be a little more flexible and cooperative than you might be inclined to be. The most important result of preparing a walk-away point is the feeling of confidence that it gives. You go into a negotiation feeling that you know where you are.   You are not at the mercy of the other side and their demands. The psychological power that it gives is well worth the time and effort.

■ *Use fall back strategy*

A colleague of mine who we will call Sandra had a call from a client about using her services for a workshop on customer services.   Sandra and the client had a long conversation about the needs of the participants and how they might structure a workshop to address these needs. Finally they came to the matter of the fee. Sandra's response was something like this, "My daily fee is $1000. However, since I have done a lot of work for you in the past I would be willing to discount this for you. How do you feel about $600?" Listen to the client's response! "Oh, that's just fine. Actually, I was going to offer you $700, but thought I might insult you with that fee." A good example of failing to use fall-back strategy effectively.

Fall-back strategy is the ability to build value into the service or product over and above the fee that you would accept. If the client cannot afford the fee, then you can proceed to "fall back" and accept less than you indicated. You can do this because you took time to build in more value than you are willing to charge for. If the client is willing to pay, well and good. However, if the client cannot or will not pay, then there is room for you to "fall back." The strategy demands that you build in enough protection that will allow you to reduce the price that you started off with.

You can't increase the price

It is a lot easier to reduce your price than to increase it in a negotiation. Actually, it is almost impossible to increase the price once you have stated it. Let's go back to the negotiation with Sandra. She is now tied to $600, although she knows that her client would gladly have paid her $700. She also knows that if her client was willing to pay $700, chances are that he would have paid more. Perhaps $750, even $800. But now her hands are tied because of a poor negotiation strategy. What should Sandra have done under the circumstances?

For starters she needs to ask a few questions that position her for justifying her normal daily rate. "How many people will be in the workshop?" she might ask. "What kind of experience do these people have in customer service activity?" would also be a good question. "What is the start time and what is the desired finish time?" These questions will alert the client to the fact that these factors challenge the skill of the workshop leader and so will affect the fee. After appropriate questions have been asked, Sandra should proceed as follows, "My normal daily fee is $1000. Since I worked with you the last time my fees have increased because of customer demand. Is your present budget able to afford my new fee?"

What this does is to start the negotiation off at the maximum figure, but leaves the door open for agreement on a lower figure. Sandra is willing to accept less. A lot less! But signalling this by actually naming the figure immediately is failing to use the advantage of fall-back strategy. Let the client name the next figure, now that you have introduced the starting figure. You just might be surprised when the client comes back with, "well we certainly enjoyed having you the last time Sandra, but we really can't afford more than $850." Sandra can hardly conceal her delight, since she was willing to go as low as $500.

How to save a deal

But what if Sandra's client comes back with an unacceptable price. What if she said, "Sandra, we did enjoy having you the last time and would love to have you again. However, our budget has been cut and I feel embarrassed to tell you, but all we have for this particular workshop is $400." Sandra is now in a spot. She is about to lose the negotiation, as this is below what she is prepared to accept. Is there anyway that this can be saved?

That depends on what Sandra is willing to accept. If her walk-away point is $500, there is still hope. She might make an arrangement to promote her album of tapes to the participants and make up for the missing $100. She may arrange for the workbooks to be printed and bound by the client. She may shorten the workshop time. The client also may have some suggestions to bridge the gap of $100 that is standing in the way of an agreement. So don't be afraid to probe and prompt the client for his ideas to help bridge the gap. When you finally reveal your bottom line figure of $500, the client may just find that extra $100 when he sees that agreement is so near.

The whole philosophy behind the fall-back strategy is to let people feel they are winning. Give them the feeling that they are getting the price down. Help them to feel that they are influencing you. But in order to achieve this objective, you must prepare by adding more value to the product and service.

Identify the benefits of the service and show how unique it is. Compare the product's features with the competition and show how it excels in performance. Boost the product and dramatize its positive factors. Do whatever you have to do to justify a high value and price. You have now set the stage for a win-win negotiation, since you are willing to retreat from your position, if the client cannot afford your initial price. Although you are retreating or "falling back," the client gets the feeling of winning, since he is getting you to reduce the price. Both sides end up feeling good.

■ Find their bottom line

"That's as far as I can go. Really that's my bottom line." That's what he said, but now it was up to us to find out if he was merely bluffing. Just as it is important that the other side does not find out our walk-away point, so it is important that we get some idea of where their walk-away point might be. If we can, we are then able to push and pressure the other side until they are close to that point. We will then be getting all that we can possibly get from that negotiation.

How to find the other side's walk-away point? You might try testing the limits by communicating finality. That means taking a risk. Communicating finality is your last chance at the end of the game, the final gambit. You could bluff and lose, but you could break through and win a significant point.

When Harry told us, "That's as far as I can go. That is my bottom line," we were in the final stages of a negotiation for our dream car. My wife and I had wanted a Chrysler New Yorker for years. Finally we had seen one that was just the right colour and the right price. We had negotiated into the area that we could afford, but we felt that there was still a further discount that the dealer could afford. We had no way of knowing this, it was just a hunch that we had. So I was bartering with Harry and asking for a further $200; which I explained was necessary to meet my financial limits.

Harry was adamant that he had gone as far as he could go, and we had to close the deal at $14,500. It was at this point that we tested the limits. My wife stood up, took her coat from the coatrack indicating she was ready to go, and said to me, "looks as if we are not going to buy a car after all." The ball was now in Harry's court. Was he really at his limit or was he bluffing? He was about to lose a sale. Was there just a little more space to move there?

Pressure, pressure and more pressure

As we rose to go, Harry quickly rose too and requested that we allow him one more chance to speak with his manager to see if there was anything that could be done. "We are so close," he said, "It would be a pity to let this nice car go." He went to the other room, spent a few minutes discussing it with his manager, and returned with a smile. "You just bought yourself a nice car Mr. and Mrs. DaCosta." We had found his bottom line! He had insisted that they were at the limit, but our test of the limits revealed that it was only a bluff. Nothing wrong with that. He was entitled to fight for a good profit margin, but we were also entitled to find the last point at which he was willing to settle. It took a lot of pressure to bring Harry to that point.

No reward without risk

Of course there was some risk on our part too. If Harry had insisted that indeed he was at the limit, and there was nothing he could do but watch us go, then we might have found ourselves in trouble too. It would be very difficult to confess we wanted to buy, but we were just trying to get $200 more off. Rather than do that we may just have walked away from the whole deal and gone to another company. And that could have meant we passed up a good deal and we may not have been able to find a similar one. Testing the limits carries risk and could mean that we lose an opportunity for agreement.

■ *Assess your power*

Power is a powerful persuader. If you have all the power in a negotiation, you probably will come out the winner. The reason is simple. You will be able to coerce the other side into submission. You will be able to force the outcome. If you have the power you can threaten, manipulate and force the other side to do the things you want them to do. I had an employer once who persuaded me to work sixty hours a week, although I had contracted for forty hours. He didn't demand this openly, but through subtle suggestions he signaled that if the work was not done, I would not have a job. The power to retain or dismiss was in his hands. There wasn't much I could do about it, except look for another job.

There are different kinds of power. There is the power of knowledge that gives you influence with others. There is the power of personal contacts that gives you the winning edge. There is the power of friendship and trust. Some of these can be used ethically and appropriately to influence others.

Having the right kind of knowledge can put you in an advantageous negotiating position. Promoting yourself as an expert in a particular field of knowledge can give credibility that will prove to be a powerful tool. Authors of books, for instance, seem to have instant credibility. If you are the author of a book you will be welcomed on radio programs, TV programs and at speaking opportunities. You have instant recognition because you are perceived to have special knowledge. "Knowledge is power" is a true maxim.

■ *Use the referral network*

One of the strongest persuaders sales people have is to make reference to someone who used their product or service and is happy about that choice. Third-party reference is one of the most reliable and powerful persuaders. If someone did this before, or used this product, or made this decision, then we want to hear about it. And when we do, we are persuaded to make the same choice.

I listened to a master persuader just recently and watched as he influenced a crowd of about one thousand people. He wanted them to buy his workshop and seminar program for learning how to sell real estate. He used the previous case scenario with great success. He told us how he had chosen people at random from previous seminars and taken them through his course at no cost to them, and they had gone on to make themselves financially independent. He told us that he had gone into cities and taken people out of unemployment lines, taken them through his course at no cost to them, and they had never gone back to the unemployment lines. He said he was prepared to chose one person out of the thousand people listening to him that day and take that person through his course at no cost to again prove that it always worked. By the time he was finished relating the many previous cases where his method had worked, he had caught the attention of all of us. He influenced us. At least 25 per cent of the audience were persuaded to invest in the course. A master persuader.

■ *Identify the issues*

Finding agreement or coming to a win-win outcome is a challenge that sometimes resembles a complex mechanical problem. If we look at a modern auto-mobile, there are so many systems with wires and tubes and valves that we get confused and hardly know where to start.

Trying to get agreement is sometimes similar in that there are so many issues that the whole affair seems to be beyond our ability to mend. If we were able to sort out the issues as we do with an automobile problem, the going might be just a little easier. When we have an automobile problem, we identify the different systems and try to decide which system has the problem. We may go through the cooling system, then look at the ignition system, or investi-gate the electrical system. We may even look at the brake system and the fuel system to see if the problem is there. Eventually we are led to the source of the problem. Similarly, in a negotiation, we must identify the different issues and see where we have common ground. We are then better able to focus on the source of the disagreement.

Only yesterday in a meeting with a potential client there was a good example of the need to identify issues. Craig and I were discussing the possibility of investing in his company. We seemed to be talking in circles. After a while it became a little frustrating. Finally I said, "Craig, let's identify the issues here. What are we really talking about? The way I see it, one issue is the viability and profitability of your company. Another issue is the financing of my investment. A third issue is the demands the company will make on my time. A fourth issue is our working relationship together and the potential of interpersonal conflict. Can you see any other issues, Craig?" His response was that he thought those were the issues that we were addressing. "Well," I said, "on the issue of potential interpersonal conflict, I think we have worked well together over the past few years, so I don't mind taking a chance on that. On the issue of time, I am prepared to give time to this agreement. So the way I see it, we really are looking at two issues only, the viability and profitability of the company and the financing of my investment. Would you agree?" "I think you are right," he said. We then focused our discussion on these two issues and tried to work out an agreement.

We moved from a frustrating and unproductive discussion to agreement. Identifying issues is often overlooked during negotiations to the eventual frustration of the participants. This results in an unsatisfactory agreement. When the issues have been identified, the first step should be to identify the common ground. This results in some positive developments. If you can show there are many areas in which you both agree, there is a sense of momentum towards an agreement. It makes both parties feel that progress is being made. It tends to help both feel more positive about the negotiation and to improve the atmosphere and climate of the proceedings.

Find common ground.

One of the advantages of identifying the issues is that you immediately become aware of the issues on which you agree. This gives momentum to the negotiation and moves it in the right direction. One of the elements of persuasion is to find the little things that you can agree on, then gradually move the discussion on to bigger challenges. A strategy used by professional negotiators in union/management negotiations is to deal first with the matters where there is likely to be compromise and agreement, and then move on to the more difficult items. The previous successes tend to put pressure on the negotiators to continue moving towards a final agreement on all issues.

■ Stop arguing forever

You never win an argument. Even if you win, you lose, and if you lose it, you lose it. "A man or woman convinced against their will, is of the same opinion still." Credit that one to a Greek sage. Through the years it has been reinforced by many modern sages. Dale Carnegie in his outstanding bestseller, **How to win friends and influence people** said, "The only way to get the best of an argument is to avoid it." Arguments, rather than solving problems, only polarize people.

▪ *Show respect*

Perhaps the single most important need of human beings today is respect. There never has been a time when the need for respect has been so important. Women are marching, special interest groups are fighting, children are complaining and nations are preparing for war, all because they feel they are not getting the respect they deserve. We may not be able to solve the world's problems, but at the personal level, we can begin to turn the tide by giving those we deal with the appropriate respect. How do we show respect? The answer has been around for 2000 years! "Do unto others as you would have them do unto you."

▪ *Watch the 55 per cent*

According to Albert Meharabian's research, 55 per cent of your message is communicated through body language. You are missing more than half of the message, if you are not sensitive to the subtle signals a person's body is sending you. Is eye contact positive? Does this person exhibit confidence through erect posture, a firm handshake and a pleasant facial expression? With good judgement and practice, we can get a pretty good picture of what is going on in another person's mind by just watching his body language.

■ *Shift mental gears.*

Most of us are preoccupied with our own interests, goals and problems. We are constantly listening to the station: WIIFM (what's in it for me.) To reach others and influence them, we need to tune into their station and become aware of what they are thinking. Rather than being preoccupied with our goals and objectives, it is more productive to be preoccupied with the other person's goals and ambitions. If we can satisfy them, we become important to them. Famous speaker Zig Ziglar says, "To the extent that you satisfy other people's needs, they will satisfy your needs."

■ *Flinch at the first offer.*

People seldom make their best offer the first time around. They usually are in an exploratory mode trying to find out just where you are. If an offer is made, your response should be a gesture of discomfort. In other words, you thought they were going to offer more. Express this. You might even want to articulate a response like, "Jim, you've got to do better than that." What this means is that you are disappointed that the offer is so low. This is your initial response. If there is more to be had, you stand a good chance of getting it. If it is their bottom line, you might have to settle for the first offer. But at least you made it understood you were expecting more.

■ *Lower their expectations.*

If you can successfully impact the expectations the other person has, you will get more of your share of the disputed area. Every negotiator has a fair idea where he or she would like the negotiation to end. This is quite often more of a wish than a plan. If we can change this "wish" in the early stages of the negotiation, we can get a better deal for ourselves. To do this we need to identify the weaknesses in their offer, dramatize them and build them into a rationale for a lower value. Presenting this rationale with conviction will successfully communicate to the other side that their expectations are too high. With lowered expectations, it is not long before actual reductions in price will take place. An adage to follow in this respect is to always start at a significantly lower price if you are in the role of purchaser. This sets the tone for the rest of the negotiation. The other party is now obligated to move you up, a challenge which is sometimes difficult.

■ *Abdicate your throne.*

If you act as if you are the king of a kingdom, the absolute expert in your field, you might find that attitude generates opposition from the other side. They just might begin to look for holes in your armour with a focus on trying to deflate you. A little modesty goes a long way. Express the possibility that you might be wrong. Ask for their help in coming to an amicable settlement. Show your willingness to compromise and meet them half way. One of the approaches I find enormously helpful when I am asking for cooperation is to begin by saying, "I wonder if you can help me." The standard answer is, "Well, I'll certainly try." Now the person is on your side, trying to find some ways in which they can be helpful to you. Can't ask for better than that.

■ *Compromise to build trust*

A piece of the pie is better than none at all. Negotiation is a matter of give and take. Be willing to give a little so that the other side is encouraged to give a little also. Any negotiation where one side is determined to take all and be the absolute winner must end in an unsatisfactory outcome. Driving a hard bargain is a short-term strategy and quite often is also a blind strategy.

For a positive and long-term relationship, you must be willing to let the other side have their fair share also. No relationship can grow to be a positive one if any side feels they are being taken advantage of. Sensible and realistic compromise builds a strong foundation of trust that will eventually lead to strong, long-term and positive relationships.

■ *Test the limits.*

Compromise does not mean to give in weakly and passively. You want to be sure that you are getting what you need to get from the negotiation. It is perfectly fair to push the other side to the point they have decided they will go to. In other words, they have a walk-away point, which is the final limit they will go to. When you have found this point, you have the best deal you can possibly get. Beyond that the other side will walk away and you will have no deal.

To reach that point you may have to take a risk and "test the limits." That means indicating you are willing to walk away if further concessions are not made. It means putting pressure on the other side to give more, or see the deal fall through. At this point no one really knows who is bluffing. If there is no more to give, and an impasse is imminent, you might have accomplished your objective. You now know that they are at their limit. It's time to close the deal.

■ *Use deadline pressure.*

One of the ways to test the limits is through deadlines. Putting a time deadline on a negotiation introduces tremendous pressure to come to some conclusion before the deadline is reached. If you can introduce a deadline into a negotiation, it forces decisions to be made under emotional pressure. This will sometimes work in your favour. If you have to leave town by a 5:10 p.m. flight and must have an answer on a purchase you have made an offer on, the seller realizes that if a decision is not made by the deadline, the deal is off.

■ *Save their face.*

A negotiator may walk away from a good deal, all because of pride or embarassment. The reason? He doesn't want to look bad. Perhaps a demand has been made for further concessions, and the other side has explained that there is no more to give. The negotiator is now put in the position of accepting something that she said was impossible to accept. Her statement was a bluff, and the other side called that bluff. She is now about to look like a liar, if she accepts. How can the deal be saved? By helping her save face. The negotiator must make an incidental concession that gives the other side a chance to say yes.

■ *Find the win-win outcome*

Taking the twists and turns necessary to finding that middle road is sometimes not easy. It means probing and asking. Certainly the technique of asking the right kinds of questions is extremely necessary. It also means being sensitive to the subtle messages coming from the other person. This means being good at reading body language. It means being able to put yourself in the other person's place and deciding whether he is considering your offer to be a good deal. All this in a spirit of respect, fairness and fun. If you can inject some humour into the communication process that is leading you towards an agreement, it's bound to have a positive effect. This, although difficult, has a great reward. A win-win outcome with all the good feeling that goes with that worthy objective.

21 Strategies for Everyday Negotiation

- Learn to read people
- Take Control
- Find your walk-away point
- Protect your territory
- Use fall back strategy
- Find their bottom line
- Assess your power
- Use the referral network
- Identify the issues
- Stop arguing forever
- Show respect
- Watch the 55 per cent
- Shift mental gears
- Flinch at the first offer

- Lower their expectations
- Abdicate your throne
- Compromise to build trust
- Test the limits
- Use deadline pressure
- Save their face
- Find the win-win outcome

Chapter 8

16 SECRETS FOR PRESENTATIONS THAT GIVE YOU VISIBILITY AND CREDIBILITY

The most important factor

One great North American speaker, Dr. Kenneth McFarland, was asked on one occasion what he thought was the most important factor in a persuasive presentation.

That is a question I like to ask audiences also. In presentation skills workshops I will ask the question, "Can you state in one word what quality is most to be desired in effective presentations?" The standard answers are: confidence, enthusiasm, clarity, knowledge, eloquence or organization.

These are all fine words and certainly very closely related to the word that Dr. Kenneth McFarland responded with. Certainly they describe qualities critical to the preparation and delivery of a good presentation. But they seem to lack that comprehensive quality Dr. McFarland's word conveys. His word is VITALITY.

Vitality is more than enthusiasm. It is a bigger word than enthusiasm. Vitality includes enthusiasm, but it also includes a lot of other qualities, such as truth, animation, life, vigour and vital force. Vitality is the quality that raises a subject from being dead and boring to the level of being vital and alive.

In a workshop I conducted, I asked a participant to give a short, three-minute presentation on a subject of his own choice. After a short preparation period, Alvin proceeded to the front of the room with a rather slow and reluctant approach. On reaching the lectern he addressed the group in a low, almost inaudible voice. Without any trace of enthusiasm or indeed any feeling at all, he said, "I would like to tell you about my hobby, which is stamp collecting. I have been a stamp collector for many years and have a number of albums."

Up until this point, Alvin had not yet looked at me or acknowledged anyone else in the audience through positive eye contact. He continued on in the same monotonous style, "Sometimes I sit down with my colleagues and exchange stories about the prices we have paid for certain stamps, or some outstanding exchange I have made for a rare stamp." As Alvin droned on, we the listeners felt sorry for him and his boring hobby. At least that's the way it seemed to us. We felt Alvin did not enjoy stamp collecting and probably used it as a means to fill up time. As the ordeal drew to an end, Alvin's voice became even more inaudible, and the last few sentences were spoken in a whisper. Alvin returned to his seat, probably feeling a little embarrassed. His entire speech lacked any semblance of vitality.

As the workshop progressed we turned to the matter of evaluating the presentations. I asked Alvin, who was now sitting at the back of the room, to share with us how he felt about his speech. "Is there anything you would change, if you had to do it over again?" I asked.

■ *Bring your subject to life*

A transformation took place in Alvin. A whole new personality emerged. Alvin's eyes lit up as he started speaking directly to me. His whole demeanour changed and his voice took on an enthusiastic and animated tone. Continuing to address me directly with hand gestures to emphasize his feelings, and facial expressions to match, he explained, "I know that I didn't convey how exciting and interesting stamp collecting has been to me. If I could just make you see the enthusiastic conversations that my colleagues and I have as we discuss the latest developments in the stamp collecting field." Alvin continued to make eye contact with me as he warmed to the subject. His voice could be heard all around the room clearly and distinctly.

The moment Alvin started to respond to my question he had the attention of everyone in the room. Just the tone of his voice with its air of urgency caught our attention. The intensity of his total message caused us to rethink our previous conclusion that stamp collecting was a boring hobby. The vitality Alvin was projecting brought his subject to life.

Alvin's first presentation to the audience was marred by lack of eye contact, monotone voice, no gestures.....in short, no vitality. His second presentation, which was a direct one-on-one communication with me, was filled with animation, enthusiasm, positive eye contact, and hand gestures emphasizing his feelings. A dramatic example of vitality.

■ *Be yourself again*

Most of us are vital and capable communicators when conversing with one person. Give us an audience of one - a good friend or perhaps a relative - and we project our personalities and our feelings with all the emotion and sincerity that get our messages across effectively. However, as soon as we stand before an audience, all the animation and vitality drains away, and we become as "boring" as Alvin.

What we need to do is to be ourselves again. If you can project the same amount of enthusiasm and animation that you project in a one-on-one situation, you will be a good presenter. Effective speaking to groups is really no different from a conversation with a good friend, except that you amplify yourself. How you communicate in a formal presentation should be much the same as the way you communicate when you talk to a single person.

Unlearning inhibitions

Dale Carnegie in his popular book **How to develop Self-Confidence and Influence People by Public Speaking** identified an important factor. He suggested that in effective speaking it's not so important that you learn new things, but rather that you try to unlearn some of the things you take on. For instance, as the average workshop participant walks to the lectern, a transformation seems to take place. A moment before, this person may have been having an animated conversation with another workshop participant. But as the person realizes she is about to stand before a roomful of people and twenty pairs of eyes are going to be focussed on her, a change occurs. With reluctant steps she drags herself to the lectern. Without any enthusiasm or eye contact she then proceeds to mumble and grumble her way through a speech. What she needs is to be herself again: the same friendly manner, the same warm expression, the same natural gestures, the same animated voice and positive eye contact.

Amplifying yourself

As you talk to an audience you must amplify yourself by expanding yourself according to the audience's size and demands. If you are talking to a group of five or ten people, you would raise your voice a little. You would also use more emphatic gestures to emphasize your points, and you would be careful to give every member of the audience eye contact.

As the audience gets bigger, you would want to amplify yourself even more to meet the demands of a larger audience. Eye contact would be expanded to acknowledge all parts of the audience, voice volume would be increased to reach everyone, and facial and hand gestures would be expanded to greatly dramatize the points you are making. But the content of your speech and the style you project should remain the same as you normally use in conversation.

Perhaps one of the greatest errors an inexperienced speaker can make is trying to be somebody else: using the voice inflections, the pacing, the style of someone else. This does not mean we can't take hints from good speakers and learn from them. What it does mean is that you must remain basically your own person.

Basics for good delivery

When we listen to a vital speech we are only aware that we are captivated by the speaker's vitality. We are so under the spell of the speaker's words that we are not aware of what the speaker is doing. We are on the crest of a great wave, carried along by the power of the speaker's eloquence and energy. If we were to stop for a moment and withdraw ourselves from the speaker's influence, we would find that there are certain critical factors present. These factors are always present in any effective presentation. They are basic to good delivery and are the tools of all good speakers. They are paramount, if you want your speech to have impact. Some of these critical factors are enthusiasm, spontaneity, eye contact, voice modulation, gestures and organization. Without these your presentation will lack vitality and become a series of words without life.

■ *Get excited about your material*

The source of enthusiasm is a real, sincere desire to communicate. You must have a strong urge to express the feelings you have about your subject. When you listen to Billy Graham, Martin Luther King Jr. or Zig Ziglar, you sense a deep and overpowering desire to communicate. They wanted to speak and this strong desire showed in the way they presented their material. Enthusiasm cannot be faked. If you really want to communicate, if you really care about the topic, your voice will have an enthusiastic quality, and your audience will hear it.

The amount of enthusiasm you project naturally is a matter of individual difference. If you are an out-going person who displays feelings openly, you may find it easy to project your enthusiasm in a speech. If you are rather reserved, your audience may not be able to pick up the more subtle signs of your enthusiasm as readily. Reserved people who seldom display feelings openly must do more in a speech than what comes naturally. They must work to intensify their feelings about what they are doing so their emotions can be communicated. Developing this intensity requires an extra effort.

One way is to make sure your topic excites you. You cannot afford to select a topic that you are only lukewarm about. The outgoing person might be able to show enthusiasm about an uninspiring topic, but the reserved person cannot. To be perceived as enthusiastic, you must be truly excited. You must be involved with the material. Develop vivid mental pictures of what you are trying to say. Mental activity will lead to physical manifestation.

Another way to project more enthusiasm is to read out loud in practice sessions. Choose a dramatic story, or poetry or some appropriate passage and read out loud. As you read, exaggerate and dramatize your expression. Where excitement is appropriate, exaggerate with voice animation; where sorrow is being expressed, adopt exaggerated mournful tones. Laugh, cry or shout as required. This exercise will tend to make you more expressive in your normal conversation and will introduce this quality into your presentations.

■ *Never memorize your speech*

Another vital factor in delivering your presentation is spontaneity. The secret of spontaneity is in how you prepare for a speech. Never memorize your speech! Never get preoccupied with words. What you want to have is mastery of content rather than mastery of words.

If I asked you to tell me how to get downtown, you would be able to tell me spontaneously because you have made the trip so many times that the knowledge is literally a part of you. However, if I asked you to tell me about the material you studied for a history class, your ability to do so spontaneously would depend on the quality of the effort you had made to master the material. If you had weighed and considered the material, if you had tried to understand the concepts rather than just memorized the details and dates, you would have enough understanding to discuss the content spontaneously.

Spontaneity is that quality that makes an idea sound as if it is being formed at the time it is spoken. It is that characteristic of voice that makes an idea sound new, and fresh and vital. Good actors can make lines they have spoken literally thousands of times sound original. They have mastered the art of spontaneity.

Since spontaneity is developed from a mastery of content rather than words, an effective exercise to improve spontaneity is to work with ideas and mental pictures rather than words. Good speakers generate vivid mental pictures. To speak confidently, with spontaneity and vitality, visualize your speech without memorizing it verbatim.

Visualization is a type of rehearsal in which you picture how the events of a presentation take place. It is nonverbal, emphasizing that too much description turns off the imaging process. Let the images form in the back of your mind, then let the description come to you. To aid in the visualization process, it is helpful to draw a series of pictures. Your pictures should just be stick figures without too much detail. Try to control the urge to use words and opt more for the imaging of pictures in your mind.

To reinforce the pictures or ideas you are visualizing in your mind, try telling a friend about them in an informal way. A good way to prepare for a presentation is to converse with a friend about what you are going to tell your audience. In doing this, you get away from a formal and unnatural style and begin to talk in a more natural, conversational and spontaneous style. The exercise also helps you to crystalize the ideas and pictures more vividly in your mind. This kind of preparation allows greater freedom of expression. It allows you to express yourself with all the spontaneity, creativity and innate humour you have.

■ *Study audience reaction*

What do you think of individuals who do not look you in the eye when they speak with you? Your attitude toward them is probably negative. In one-on-one communication we expect speakers to look at us while they are talking. When speakers do not look at us, we lose our need to look at them and our desire to pay attention to them. The result is a break in the communication bond and proportional loss of attention. As a speaker, you maintain a certain amount of control over your listener's attention simply by looking at them. But not only does good eye contact help attention, it also increases audience confidence in the speaker. When speakers look you in the eye, you are probably more willing to trust them.

As you gain skill in speaking, you will become aware of the most beneficial aspect of good eye contact. That is your ability to study audience reaction to what you are saying. Communication is a two-way street. You are speaking with an audience, and it in turn is speaking to you. In daily conversation response is verbal, while in public speaking response is shown by various cues. People who are virtually on the edges of their seats with their eyes on you are paying rapt attention. An audience yawning, looking out the window, and slouching is saying "we are bored."

You can determine what adjustments you need to make by being aware of audience reaction. As you gain greater skill, you will be able to make more and better use of the information learned through eye contact.

How do you maintain eye contact with an audience? It is, of course, physically impossible to look at your entire audience at once. What you can do is talk with individuals and small groups in the audience. Do not spend all of your time looking front and centre. The people at the ends of aisles and those in the back of the room are every bit as important as those right in front of you.

Develop a vital and commanding voice

Your voice has all the capabilities of a musical instrument. How you use it makes the difference between success or failure. You can use the qualities of pitch, pace and power to develop an expressive, vital and commanding voice, or you can settle for a flat, monotonous and boring voice. The difference is in the level of variation that you inject into these characteristics of pitch, pace and power.

Very few people speak in a true monotone, but many limit themselves severely by using only two or three tones and relatively unchanging power and pace. The effect of an actual or near monotone is that the audience is lulled to sleep. Without vocal cues to assess the comparative value of words, members of an audience will usually lose interest. (see page 51 for a strategy for adding vitality to your voice.)

■ *Use Gestures normally*

Quite often participants in workshops say, "I am not a very expressive person, and I don't normally speak with my hands." It is interesting that when people are discussing this subject with me in a private conversation, they are quite often expressing themselves with their hands and facial expressions, contradicting the very words they are saying at the time.

One memorable incident in a workshop comes to mind where a participant was expressing a thought to the rest of the workshop participants. "I know that there are some cultures that tend to be very expressive with their hands," he said. "However, my background and culture tends to downplay expressive hand gestures, and rather stress the importance of effective word usage and intellect." He continued on in this vein, and as he warmed to his subject and expanded on the point he was making, I noticed, and indeed the other participants began to notice too, that he was actually contradicting himself as he spoke. To emphasize the points he was making, he was using strong hand gestures as well as meaningful facial expressions.

This went on for a short time, when one of the group spoke up and said, "But you are doing the very thing that you are criticizing." His immediate reply was, "No, I'm not." It was not until the whole class insisted that he had been using natural hand gestures and facial expressions that he was convinced he had been using the very style he was criticizing. Just an example of the fact that we all tend to use gestures normally!

Normal use of gestures is what is required. If you stop using your hands in the way you normally use them, you will give the impression of being stilted and uncaring. Some inexperienced speakers have a problem with their hands. They end up putting them in their pockets, holding them behind, or in front of them, or sometimes even folding them. If you find yourself in any of these situations, try placing your hands on the lectern as you speak. If you are speaking without a lectern, just leave them by your sides. This way your hands will be free to help you emphasize a point.

Don't be afraid to role play a situation. If you are talking about skiing, bend your knees and take on the role of a skier. If you are in a business meeting, explaining the need for positive reinforcement, role play the voice tones and posture of the manager. If you are describing a dramatic example to emphasize a point, use your body to illustrate the details and your voice to mimic the characters in your example. The audience is then able to see and follow your story more easily, and the role play makes it more interesting.

Good speakers are always on the move. They hardly ever stand still behind the lectern. They move into and away from the audience. At one time they are talking to one side of the audience then, suddenly their focus shifts to the other side of the audience. They are constantly moving, adding vitality and excitement to their presentations.

Organizing a speech

If you organize your thoughts, establish your purpose and illustrate your points, you will make it easy for your audience to follow your presentation and they will listen to you.

I listened to a keynote speaker at a convention recently, and he was a master at his craft. First he told us what he was going to tell us, then he told us, then he told us what he had told us. He illustrated his points with examples, with statistics and surveys, and personal experiences. He ended with a call for action.

Organization is clear thinking. Organization is a way of putting your ideas in an orderly manner so that your listeners find it easy to follow. In some respects, it is doing the work for your listeners. If your points are not specific and illustrated, your listeners will not organize it in their own minds. They will wander off mentally, and think their own thoughts. Thinking requires energy, and your audience is not about to do your work for you. They came to hear you with the expectation that you have done all the work. They are there to get the benefit of your knowledge, put into a framework of important ideas, supported with examples and personal experiences.

How often have you sat in a meeting and found your thoughts wandering away, because the speaker was vague and abstract in his presentation and was utterly uninteresting, because he had not personalized his speech? So regard organizing your speech as working for your audience. You must clearly identify the key points of your subject for your audience, and then lead them logically toward an acceptable solution.

Listening to a well-organized presentation is comparable to watching a movie on the screen. If the objective and purpose is clear, if the points are vividly described with picture words, the audience sees the presentation and enters into the experience with the speaker. Some of the most memorable speeches I have heard were speeches where the speaker described the experience in such an effective way that we, the audience, were there with him and experienced it with him.

To improve your organization and keep your audience interested we need three important factors: effective visualization, quantified descriptions and supporting evidence.

■ *Picture the events of a speech*

Organized thinking develops from effective visualization. Try to picture the events of a speech in your mind. Emphasize the pictures rather than the words. Visualization is a type of exercise where the emphasis is on the pictures. Let the images form in the back of your mind, then let the description come to you. It is a nonverbal activity. If you can feel the bite of the wind; the sting of the freezing rain; if you can hear the thick juicy T-bone steaks sizzling on the grill; if you can see the golden rays of a sunset shining through scattered clouds, you will be able to describe these sensations vividly and confidently.

But more importantly, your audience will see and experience the sensations also. One of the cardinal rules of persuasion is to be crystal clear in your communication. If your audience can see and experience your thoughts as you relay them, they will be far more inclined to follow you. On the other hand, if they are doubtful about your intentions because of disorganized and sloppy thinking, they will turn off and delay decisions.

■ *Get beyond the adjectives*

When someone describes a situation to us, we have to get beyond the adjective to find out how much of that characteristic is present. It's not enough to know that something is strong, or durable, or economical, or tasty or desirable. We want to know how strong, how durable, how economical, how tasty or how desirable it is. We need to quantify its value.

Can you see yourself saying, "I don't see any reason for buying from John Doe Inc. as their price is higher than what we are now paying. Even though they give better service, I don't think the difference is worth it." Everything needs to be quantified here. How much higher is the price? What does the service consist of? Are deliveries more often on time? Is the packaging better? And for all these questions, how much better? And still a further question, how much does it matter?

A good rule of thumb in trying to quantify is to get a number in place of an adjective or adverb where you can. Where it isn't feasible to get a number, work towards it by estimating quantities. Don't use the word "soon" if you can reasonably say, "By next week." And if you are not sure it will be next week, extend your range another month. Meticulous regard for reliable and proven evidence will establish you as a clear thinker. On the other hand, ideas presented without the benefit of strong, supportive evidence will quickly brand you as a casual and careless speaker.

■ *Support your point with evidence*

Evidence is the bridge that joins an abstract statement to individuals in the audience. The statement, "good health is necessary to enjoy life," needs to have evidence to focus it and make it more meaningful to an individual. A personal experience would supply this focus. For instance, "I have a friend who suffered a minor heart attack some months ago and through this experience, learned to appreciate his health a lot more." Evidence can take many forms such as personal experiences, analogies, judgements of experts, examples, statistics and facts, appropriate anecdotes, quotations and demonstrations. Support your points with strong evidence and your audience will respond with rapt attention.

The secret of good organization

To keep your speech organized, always "tell people what you are going to tell them, then tell them, then tell them what you told them." In the introduction of your presentation you "tell them what you are going to tell them," in the body of your presentation you "tell them" and in the conclusion you "tell them what you told them." If you keep your presentations broken down into these three separate parts, you will be more interesting and your audience will follow you more easily.

■ Should you open with a joke?

The introduction of your speech is when you get attention. Examples of good openings might be a startling question or a challenging statement, an appropriate quotation, a suitable anecdote or a display of some object or picture. Should you open with a joke? If the joke is unrelated to your subject, and the intent is just to "warm up" the audience, the answer is emphatically "NO." To pull in an unrelated joke is unprofessional, and a sophisticated audience will resent it. If, however, your humorous story relates to your topic and leads into your subject, it might be acceptable. You will have to judge as you analyze the audience, your subject and the occasion. Be sure your introduction "tells them what you are going to tell them." Too many speakers are five or ten minutes into their speeches and the audience is still asking the question, "What is she talking about?" Give an overview of your subject, or define the problem you intend to address, and tell the audience the direction your speech will take.

■ *Don't use too many points*

The body of your speech is where you "tell them." This is where the great bulk of information is presented. This is where you state your facts, present your proof and refute opposing views. The body of your speech must support your opening statement or objective and supply the evidence that conclusively proves the stand you take on your topic. It is where you examine the alternatives and show the absolute logic of your perspective.

Because the information is so profuse in this part of your speech, it is critical that you keep it organized. Identify your points clearly, keep them separate and illustrate them with appropriate evidence. Mixing separate points, using abstract statements and failing to illustrate are the bane of poor speakers. Another formula for failure is to use too many points. Information overload will turn off your listeners. They are just not able to process it, particularly if it is in a disorganized format.

■ *Call for action*

In your conclusion you "tell people what you told them." This is the end of your presentation. The audience is aware you have supplied all the evidence and proven your case. This is your chance to call for action. Tell the audience what you want them to do as a result of your presentation. Take time now to review the major points you have presented. Summarize succinctly the main arguments and close the case convincingly. Respond to the unarticulated question the audience is asking: "So what? Why have you taken the time and made the effort to prove this case to us. What do you want us to do?"

A work of art

A well-organized speech is a work of art. It flows from a poised and professional appearance to an interesting, attention-getting and effective introduction. It continues on to specific points ably supported by appropriate evidence and ends on a dramatic note with a realistic call for action. Any effort and energy expended in achieving these results are justified.

North America's number One fear

In a survey taken a few years ago, public speaking was cited as the number One fear in North America. Amazingly, people actually put the fear of public speaking ahead of the fear of heights, insects and bugs, divorce, and even death. Small wonder that 80 per cent of the people that come to seminars on public speaking come for the sole purpose of getting rid of their nervousness. "Are there any techniques to help me get rid of sweaty palms, shaky knees and butterflies in my stomach?" they ask. How can I look even reasonably confident and communicate my ideas in a professional way? Is it possible to get rid of nervousness, or will it always be with me? Are good platform speakers nervous? How is it that they look so confident?

Good news

The good news is that some excellent platform speakers still confess to being nervous. The good news is that you too can look just as confident as a professional speaker. And the best news of all is that you can control your nervousness, you can learn to give an effective speech, and you can leave the lectern feeling good about the presentation you have given. In short, you can learn to enjoy public speaking.

Controlling nervousness

Nervousness is destructive! The world is full of people who, when they have opportunities, turn away from them because they are not able to control nervousness. Over and over again in seminars, participants tell of times when promotions or other opportunities were offered, and they refused, because they were not able to handle the public speaking that went along with those promotions or opportunities. Finally, they came to themselves and decided that somehow, somewhere they would face up to their nervousness and win.

Vernon Duncan is a good example of facing up to nervousness and winning. Vernon experienced the same kind of nervousness and fear the average person shows. In his younger years, he avoided social gatherings where he had to express ideas to more than one or two persons. At his work he contributed nothing in meetings, although his ideas were just as creative and workable as any other. He was overcome with fear that others would laugh at the suggestions he might make. So he played it safe. He said nothing.

Gradually, he began to realize that he would forever be stuck in the uninteresting and dead-end job he was in. He began to see that if he never got out of his shell to tell the world about all those marvellous and unique ideas swimming around in his mind, no one would ever know they were there. And, of course, he would never get any credit for them. So Vernon decided he had to find a way to get out of himself and start to communicate with others.

One of the books he was reading in his desperate search for help talked about Toastmasters International. The author emphasized that the organization offered a program for self-development. It promised dramatic improvement in communication skills, and it promised a positive and supportive environment for inexperienced speakers. Vernon decided to give it a try. After all, what could he lose!

Vernon's contact with Toastmasters was the beginning of good things for him. He found a supportive, encouraging group of people willing to do anything they could to help. Vernon was encouraged to get involved in simple exercises that helped him to think on his feet and to get used to speaking to more than one or two people. Vernon Duncan now enjoys speaking to people. He is never happier than when he has an audience to speak to. People pay him to speak and adjust programs to suit his schedule.

Not everyone wants to be a Vernon Duncan. Not everyone wants to speak to large audiences and travel over the world. But all of us do want to speak effectively and confidently. All of us do want to say a few words at a wedding reception or social gathering. All of us do want to present our ideas at a business meeting or convention with the conviction and confidence that will make others listen. And all of us can do it!

■ *Picture yourself with friends*

If I were to ask you to talk to a good friend right now about your area of expertise, you probably would welcome the opportunity to express your depth of knowledge on the subject. You would hardly pause to think of where you would start. It probably would all come to you in a format that would allow you to explain it effectively. If I were to ask you immediately after you had talked to your friend to talk on the same subject to an audience of 100 of your peers, what would happen? Would you immediately freeze? Would sweaty palms and shaky knees be evident? Would you begin to worry about how you would present your story? Most of us can speak eloquently to one person, but as soon as we are asked to speak to an audience of more than one, we get symptoms of extreme fear. And it is very evident that this fear is generated because the audience has changed from being one person to 20 or 50 or more.

Audiences are made up of individuals. It was easy to talk to a friend. Now you have 10 more friends to talk to. They are just as normal, friendly and predictable as one friend was. Actually, an audience is even more predictable, because an audience is always on your side. How often do you listen to a speech with the hope that the speaker will fail? In most instances, you are hoping the speaker will be in good form, and that you will benefit from the experience. So one of the most important factors in

getting control of your nervousness is to begin to
see your audience as friendly. See them as a group
of individuals, much like the people you talk with
everyday in your job or in your community.

■ *Prepare and practise*

When you watch and listen to a good speaker, his
or her presentation seems effortless. Words and
ideas flow together in an easy, natural way. You
are able to follow easily the concepts and the
information the speaker is expressing. Your attention becomes focussed and your interest is captured.
Behind such a performance is a secret. A secret the
audience may not be aware of. A secret called
PREPARATION.

Careful preparation is one of the most important
factors in controlling nervousness. The knowledge
you have done your research, organized your speech
and rehearsed your presentation will bolster your
confidence and strengthen your nerve. In a recent
public speaking course, I asked June Wild to have
a speech prepared for the next session. June arrived
on time, but expressed reservations about being able
to give the speech. She said she felt "awfully nervous." I talked with her, trying to encourage her to
make the effort. As we talked, I discovered that she
had had a busy week and no time to prepare. Her
nervousness was compounded by the fact she was
not prepared. I encouraged her to take time during
the coming week to do some preparation. "Do some
reading on your subject," I suggested. "Talk to a
friend and tell her what you would like to tell us in

your speech. Use your tape recorder and listen to yourself during a rehearsal session. Try going through your speech two or three times before you come back to the course next week." It sounded like a lot of work, but I told her the result would be worth it. She would feel much better about the speech and she would have her nervousness under control.

June returned the week after to give her speech and gave a superb performance. She thanked me for encouraging her to take time to prepare. "It made the world of difference," she said. "I listened to myself on my tape recorder and changed the things I didn't like. I also talked to a friend about what I was going to say and that made me feel more comfortable with my topic."

Preparation does not always mean numerous visits to the library and long nights spent in reading and researching your topic. Your topic might be something you are thoroughly familiar with. It might be a topic you are involved in daily and minutely. Further research may not be necessary. However, you must take time to put your knowledge into an organized framework. You must develop your concepts, identify your points, illustrate them with examples and personal experiences, and you must tie them all together with a theme your audience can follow.

Preparation never means memorizing your speech. One of the greatest mistakes inexperienced speakers make is to develop the habit of memorizing their speeches. A memorized speech may appear to be a guarantee against nervousness, but it's a mirage. Forget one word or one line of your speech, and you might forget everything. Never memorize a speech verbatim. Focus on ideas and vivid mental pictures. Visualize your speech. Preparation through the visualization techinque allows greater freedom of expression. It will make you feel better about yourself and heighten your confidence.

■ *Don't be afraid to be afraid*

President Roosevelt warned his nation with words that have now become immortal, ".....the only thing we have to fear, is fear itself." Helen Hayes, one of the most respected names in the history of the American stage said, "....on the day after the night when I fail to become nervous, that is the day on which I will retire from the stage."

Many of the great performers, actors, and speakers confess to a small amount of nervousness. They say they would not want to completely overcome it because it actually helps them to rise to their full potential. It gets the adrenalin flowing and prepares them for peak performance. Accept your nervousness as a positive force in helping you to make better presentations. Understand that it is something that can help you rather than hinder you. Convince yourself that all you need to do is to control it.

■ *Speak as often as you can*

When Vernon Duncan made his second speech he found that his nervousness was not as acute as it was while making his first speech. When he made his third speech he found that his nervousness was not as evident as while making his second speech. Indeed, he began to notice that each successive speech was easier in the sense that his nervousness decreased with each speech. He became less and less apprehensive about giving speeches, and more and more confident that he would be successful. Eventually, Vernon developed to the level that when preparing for a speech, thoughts of nervousness didn't bother him anymore. Rather, he began to anticipate speaking more with a feeling of excitement and enthusiasm, than with a feeling of fear. He actually began to enjoy the experience.

Vernon found out a simple, commonsense fact. The more we speak, the less inhibited and nervous we are. Public speaking is just like any other skill.....the more we do it, the more comfortable we become.

16 Secrets for Effective Presentations

- Bring your subject to life

- Be yourself again

- Get excited about your material

- Never memorize your speech

- Study audience reaction

- Use gestures normally
- Picture the events of a speech
- Get beyond the adjectives
- Support your point with evidence
- Should you open with a joke?
- Don't use too many points
- Call for action
- Picture yourself with friends
- Prepare and practise
- Don't be afraid to be afraid
- Speak as often as you can

Chapter 9

10 WAYS TO INCREASE SELF-WORTH, PERSONAL CONFIDENCE, SERENITY AND REAL SUCCESS

How others see us

When was the last time you took a family picture? Or even a group picture at a picnic or other event? When the pictures came back from the store who did you look for first?

If your answer was anybody other than yourself, you are probably not being completely honest. Most of us, when we look at a photograph that includes ourselves, generally look first for ourselves. We want to see if our smile is right, or if the clothes we are wearing are appropriate. We want to see how we compare with others in the picture. We are concerned about what others see and what others think about us.

I can remember the first full-length pants that I wore as a child. Although it goes back many years, I can still vividly remember the concern I had that the seams were not falling where they should. I must have been quite a sight to the adults around me as, at that young age, I tried to keep the seams of my pants directly in line with the toes of my shoes. I walked with my eyes focussed on the toes of my shoes, all the while trying to make sure that every step was perfect. The things we do to make others think better of us!

William James, the father of psychology in America, said it best when he declared "We have a craving to be appreciated". A lot of our time is spent in activities directed at winning the attention, appreciation and approval of others. So, we tend to look at ourselves first in any pictures that include us.

How we see ourselves

Far more important than how others see us however, is how we see ourselves. We may look extraordinarily good to others, and then to ourselves we are quite unacceptable and ugly. How others see us is quite often different from how we see ourselves.

In the public speaking workshops I lead, some participants will go to the front of the room and present excellent speeches on their activities at work or on some other topic. After making the presentation, these people will confess they were nervous and uncomfortable and felt they had done a poor job. They saw themselves as failing, when all the time we were looking on in admiration at the excellent job they were doing. This is constantly happening all around us in the sense that we look at others and think they are doing well, while they are thinking of themselves as incomplete and unsuccessful. They have so much going for them, but they still insist they are failures. Their internal pictures of themselves are distorted and wrong. They have chosen to highlight the weaknesses and disregard their strengths. They have created caricatures of themselves instead of portraits.

■ *Take a look at yourself*

Let's get something straight right now. The personal picture you carry in your mind of yourself is a profoundly important and potentially magnificent tool. It drives all the decisions in your life. Indeed it is responsible for the major shifts and the ultimate direction your life will take.

The people you associate with, the career you choose, even the person you marry are all outcomes of that picture. The way you walk, the way you talk and the clothes you wear are messages that tell of the personal picture you are nurturing in your mind of yourself. It would not be an exaggeration to say your personal picture is the most important picture in your life.

Let's take a moment to see what your personal picture looks like. On the next page there is a list of factors you can measure yourself by to get some idea of how you feel about yourself. Take a moment to mark each one on the scale of 1 - 10. Don't deliberate too much about this. Spontaneously record how you feel about yourself as you think of the activity and how it relates to you. This is not an exam. It's just a simple and informal way of looking at yourself to see how you feel about yourself. After you have marked each factor, join the marks with a line from top to bottom of the page and you will then have a profile suggesting your strengths and weaknesses.

SELF-WORTH PROFILE

	1	2	3	4	5	6	7	8	9	10
Energy level	.	.	.	.	.	.	.	.	.	.
Enthusiasm	.	.	.	.	.	.	.	.	.	.
Communication	.	.	.	.	.	.	.	.	.	.
Understands people	.	.	.	.	.	.	.	.	.	.
Planning ability	.	.	.	.	.	.	.	.	.	.
Use of creativity	.	.	.	.	.	.	.	.	.	.
Persuasiveness	.	.	.	.	.	.	.	.	.	.
Determination	.	.	.	.	.	.	.	.	.	.
Understands self	.	.	.	.	.	.	.	.	.	.
Ambition	.	.	.	.	.	.	.	.	.	.
Concern for others	.	.	.	.	.	.	.	.	.	.
Self-motivation	.	.	.	.	.	.	.	.	.	.
Time management	.	.	.	.	.	.	.	.	.	.
Aspiration for excellence	.	.	.	.	.	.	.	.	.	.
Self-discipline	.	.	.	.	.	.	.	.	.	.
Problem solving	.	.	.	.	.	.	.	.	.	.
Self-confidence	.	.	.	.	.	.	.	.	.	.
Charisma	.	.	.	.	.	.	.	.	.	.
Self-development	.	.	.	.	.	.	.	.	.	.
Interest in career	.	.	.	.	.	.	.	.	.	.
Emotional control	.	.	.	.	.	.	.	.	.	.
Public speaking ability	.	.	.	.	.	.	.	.	.	.
Positive attitudes	.	.	.	.	.	.	.	.	.	.
Work with others	.	.	.	.	.	.	.	.	.	.
Decision-making skill	.	.	.	.	.	.	.	.	.	.

This is the personal picture you are carrying of yourself each day. This is the picture that is driving all of your life decisions. This is the picture that has brought into your life all the things you have today. If your life is not what you would like it to be, the picture is responsible.

■ *Beware of negative pictures*

A negative picture will drive you to discouragement, despair and ultimate disaster. I have a vivid experience of this. I was only eleven years old when the power of a negative picture expressed itself in my experience. At school one day I was in the middle of a group of boys around my own age. One of them casually commented on the size of my ears. For a moment all the boys in the group examined my ears with critical eyes. Someone jokingly said my ears looked a bit like "elephant ears" and maybe that would be a good name to give me. There was general laughter in the group and then the laughter subsided and the subject was dropped.

Dropped by everyone but me! I ran home as soon as I could and where do you think I went first? Yes, the mirror to examine the ears I had not been very conscious of before. I could clearly see what they were talking about. Indeed my ears were large and did tend to stick out prominently like an elephant. Maybe the name "elephant ears" was justified. That night I went to bed worrying about my dilemma. Why did it have to happen to me?

Preoccupation with my larger than normal ears set in. I became obsessed with my ugly ears. Everywhere I went I could see people looking at my ears. Every conversation I saw taking place was a discussion about my ears. I could even see people in the distance laughing at my ears. I couldn't hear what they were saying, but I knew those loud laughs were directed at me and my ugly ears.

It wasn't long before I began to withdraw from these groups that were talking about and laughing at my ears. I found every excuse to hide myself in my room and avoid those whose company I had enjoyed only a few weeks before. I became a recluse. I was ugly, you see, and the only way to cope with that was to hide myself away where no one would see me.

That was many years ago. I still have the same set of ears, but now they have gone back to playing the role they played before that unfortunate comment. Two normal ears doing the job of hearing. Amazing what a negative, personal picture can do to your behaviour.

When you imagine yourself as ugly it's not long before you begin to imagine others as ugly too. The distorted picture you have of yourself begins to affect your vision of others around you. You see them as having all the failings and weaknesses you think you have. Your extreme view begins to transform your world into a forest of angry, ugly and frustrated individuals. You begin to exhibit fear and suspicion. Your world begins to fill up with ugly people. And where do you think it all started? With the ugly, personal picture you developed of yourself. You created your own ugly world.

■ *Use your greatest gift*

The greatest gift we have as human beings is the ability to change the personal picture we carry in our minds. One of the most famous statements of psychologist William James is: "The greatest discovery of my generation is that human beings can alter their lives by altering their attitudes of mind."

My friend Gerry Robert is a living example of personal change through positive, personal pictures in his mind. In his best-selling book **"Conquering Life's Obstacles,"** Gerry tells his story: "I grew up in a home with a father who suffered from alcoholism. We lived in "the project," a fancy name for low-rental development, rampant with crime, drugs and violence. At ten years of age, adults encouraged me to steal. I didn't let them down. I enjoyed the attention.

In the years that followed things grew worse, considerably worse. At thirteen, a friend showed me some white pills he had bought with money from a stolen purse. They made me forget the pain. During the "trip" I didn't think about what was happening. I could escape for a while. I fell in love with "intoxication." I was in that condition as frequently and as intensely as I could be, even at that young age. I was drinking in bars at fifteen and was kicked out of school that year too and I started working full-time just before my sixteenth birthday.

I had my first run-in with the police that year. I was arrested and convicted for grand theft auto. By the time I was eighteen, I had commited many crimes including shoplifting, kidnapping, drug trafficking, abduction and armed robbery.

In February, 1977, I was arrested for armed robbery. *On September 6, 1977, however, my life was turned around forever. It is a day I will never forget! On that day, I left the life of crime and deceit. I got off the road of failure and got on the road of success. I left negative thinking behind and chose positive thinking instead.* On that very special day, I began to change from a life of destruction, despair and poverty to enjoy a life of value, happiness and prosperity."

Powerful words! Words of hope and faith and victory. As Gerry Robert says, if he can do it, so can any of us on this planet. The sequel to Gerry's remarkable story is that today he is endorsed by people like Dr. Norman Vincent Peale, Dr. Robert Schuller and other outstanding personalities. I know Gerry personally, and I know that he has transformed his life from violence and ugliness to a life of prosperity, happiness and love. All because he used his greatest gift to change the pictures of himself from failure to success.

The strangest secret

Do you want to build a life of prosperity and victory? A fuller, richer and more rewarding experience? Then listen now and listen carefully. You need to consciously and carefully build the kind of personal picture that will help you reach this goal. The resources to accomplish this magnificent task already exist. The human mind is like rich garden soil, waiting to work on what you put into it. If you put in negative, ugly thoughts, it will take them and grow you a garden full of weeds, discouragement and frustration. If you put positive and beautiful, personal pictures, it will return confidence, pride and personal success. It's all in what you put into it.

Earl Nightingale, one of the giants of this century authored an audio tape which he called **The Strangest Secret.** It has the reputation of being the only talk recording ever to win a Gold Record. Earl Nightingale searched for many years to find what he considered to be the secret of a successful life. He interviewed the great personalities of his day and read the autobiographies of the historic greats. Finally, he came back to the simple formula that has always been there. It is spoken of in the Bible and indeed in all the sacred books over the centuries. Throughout all history the great wise men and women, teachers, philosophers and prophets have agreed on this one simple formula. The strangest secret is: WE BECOME WHAT WE THINK ABOUT.

What you put into your mind will eventually express itself in your life. It is a law of the Universe. We cannot avoid it! The secret is wonderful news for some of us, and for others it is like the tolling of a bell of distress. For despite all the assurances that "what we sow we shall surely reap," there are millions, perhaps billions who will continue to sow thoughts of despair and defeat. They will continue to participate in a formula that can only take them further and further into the despair they are trying to avoid.

■ *Sow seeds of success*

For positive thoughts to take root and begin to produce the kind of experiences and reality in your life that you desire, you need to know how to sow the seed correctly. Farmers know there is a right time to sow. Likewise, there is a right time and a right way to sow the seeds of success in that magnificent machine, your mind.

In your normal, active, alert state of mind the conditions are not right for "sowing seed." The stress factor is high, and there are many barriers to prevent the "seed" getting to the level in your mind where it will "germinate" and begin to grow roots. In this state, which scientists call the Beta state, the electrical impulses in your brain are at maximum intensity, and the ability to relax and concentrate is quite difficult.

One of the phenomena of the brain is that the intensity of the electrical impulses can be changed by conscious will. These changes result in changes of consciousness. For instance in Beta, we are fully alert, thinking, talking and conversing. The other end of the spectrum is the Delta state which is a state of deep sleep. During the Delta state electrical activity has almost disappeared. We are completely unconscious. Even the brain activity of dreaming has ceased. Between Beta and Delta, there are the Alpha and Theta states where electrical activity is lower than the Beta state.

Just as a farmer loves the spring with its moisture, warmth and sunshine, so you should love the Alpha state if you want to grow some positive results in your life. It is in Alpha that the brain is relaxed, and thoughts begin to take root and influence our feelings, motivation and attitudes. The Alpha state opens the gate to our powerful Unconscious Mind where we store our life memories.

We experience the Alpha state every day and sometimes many times in a day. Every time you fall asleep you pass through the Alpha state. When you wake up you pass through the Alpha state. Alpha is the time just before you pass into the sleep state when you are completely relaxed, but your mind is still conscious. In this state electrical energy in your brain is reduced, and both your body and mind are relaxed. With practice you can bring your mind to a literal standstill and experience a calm, tranquil and serene condition. It is in this state and condition we absorb positive information more effectively and begin to impact and overwhelm the reservoir of negative conditioning that may already exist.

Here are some proven steps for achieving the Alpha state:

1. Sit in a comfortable position, hands on your lap and both feet on the floor.

2. Close your eyes.

3. Begin to form a beautiful picture in your mind. Recall a quiet, serene scene that you have experienced. It might be a moment beside a calm lake. It might be a walk through the woods on a beautiful fall day. It might be beside a rushing stream where you sat all by yourself. Allow the scene to engross and overwhelm you as it did at the time you experienced it. Enjoy the experience again and retain the picture for a few minutes.

4. You might find your mind wandering away from the experience. Don't be upset with yourself, just keep bringing your mind back to your beautiful place. Be persistent, patient and kind with yourself.

5. Now gently replace the image in your mind with a picture of the kind of person you would like to be. It might be a picture of you heading your own company or business. It might be a picture of you winning a desired trophy or prize. It might be a picture of you laughing and happy with friends around you. Whatever you have decided is a worthwhile and achievable goal, plant that seed in your mind.

6. Hold this picture in your mind for a minimum of 60 seconds.

7. Do this at least twice a day. More than that will increase the potential for good things to happen, so don't be afraid to spend more time at it.

As you continue these activities you will find it is easier for you to believe your goal will be achieved.

Try to support this development by acting as if the pictures you are entertaining have come true. William James, Harvard Professor and America's best known psychologist maintains, "We need only sincerely act as if the thing in question were real, and it will infallibly end by growing into such a connection with our life that it will become real."

■ *Use synthetic experience*

Another phenomenon of the unconscious mind is that it cannot tell the difference between a real event or experience and the same event or experience vividly imagined in your mind. The unconscious mind treats both activities the same and responds to them in similar fashion.

For instance, think about and visualize the following situation now. You are going over to your refrigerator, and you are taking out a lemon that you bought yesterday. You are cutting the lemon into four equal pieces. You are taking one of the pieces, putting it into your mouth and biting into it. You feel the tart, acid lemon juice burning your tongue and the sides of your mouth.

Now, would it be safe to say that you are vividly aware of your salivary glands working overtime? But where is the lemon juice? Only in your mind! Your unconscious mind interpreted the mental experience as if it were a real experience and gave the required response. More saliva!

Here is another example supported by many surveys

and tests done over the years. Psychologists, using controlled experimental conditions, found that mental practice could help people throw darts accurately. Their subjects sat each day in front of the target imagining they were throwing darts at it. It improved their aim as much as actually throwing the darts. How can darts and lemon juice help us in our search for greater self-confidence and success? The answer is in using "synthetic experience."

We gain confidence by small achievements. As we repeat an activity, we improve performance and our confidence level rises. In the field of public speaking, for instance, most people have a real fear approaching dread for this activity. But if people can be persuaded to speak often, their confidence will begin to rise as a result of the many successful achievements. The story of "synthetic experience" is that perhaps they don't have to literally speak often. *They could vividly imagine themselves speaking.* They could see themselves in the theatre of their minds addressing an audience successfully. They could "synthetically" see themselves as public speakers. The unconscious mind, interpreting this as the real experience, will begin to generate the self-confidence that would ordinarily come from the real experience.

Does this work? Try it and see. The testimony of hundreds and thousands of successful people is that it works like a charm. You can synthetically experience anything you want and get the results you would get from the actual experience. The only qualifying factor is the extent to which you internalize and believe the picture. Casual internalization and belief results in casual results, but results nevertheless. Absolute internalization and belief translates into absolute results.

Gerry Robert used "synthetic experience" to turn his life around. He didn't have much to draw on when he was in prison, so he had to create a new world with synthetic experiences. The happiness and prosperity he craved was certainly not a reality in his life, and he had no way of experiencing that literally. So he gave himself synthetic experiences that in turn resulted in attitudes and opportunities, which eventually resulted in what he has today. You can too!

■ *Prepare your good list now*

My first introduction to a good list was some years ago by a colleague of mine. Then more recently I was reminded of it by a participant in a workshop. We were talking about ways in which we could raise our confidence level and feel better about ourselves. I asked for activities and real life experiences that had been helpful. "I use a good list," said Tracy.

She then proceeded to tell us her good list consisted of everything she could think of that was nice about herself. On her list she put all the little achievements she had experienced over the years: finishing school, learning to drive, getting a job, and the other incidental things we tend to overlook. She said this list helped her to recognize she is an achiever. When in doubt or tending to despair, she would take it out, look at it and remind herself of her achievements.

Study after study has revealed that a preoccupation with your strengths rather than your weaknesses is more productive. Nevertheless, we sometimes deliberately prepare a "bad list" and become preoccupied with it.

We may not make a literal list, but we continue to harbour pictures of times we failed or weaknesses we have. We recall we didn't make the athletic team at school, we didn't get a place on the school band, and we didn't get the promotion we had our eyes on. We see ourselves in the losing role most of the time and reinforce our personal picture of a loser.

Why not take your pen in hand right now and begin a good list? Start with the little things. What about that book you finally read? Or the person you gave a helping hand to at the office? Or the warm "thank you" that you gave the waiter at the restaurant? Make a list of all the little things you do everyday that express the better you. Get taken up with those things, and stop worrying and thinking about the other things where you didn't quite make it. Don't give those "failures" any place in your thinking, except to say with a positive attitude, "I'll do better next time."

Here's a little line that has meant a lot to me: *Never let yesterday, use up today.* Never let the failures and losses of yesterday rear their ugly heads today to discourage and beat you down. Yesterday is gone. Today is a new day with new opportunities to reach out towards that noble goal for yourself.

■ *Choose your friends carefully*

There is an old saying I heard repeated so many times in my youth it now is a part of me. "Birds of a feather, flock together." Dad and Mom must have told me that a hundred times. They saw my inclination to hang out with the wrong kinds of people.

It was only as the years went by I really understood what they were trying to tell me. If you stay with people who are negative, critical and narrow-minded, it will only be a matter of time before you become like them. If you hang around with people who are goal oriented, positive and successful, you can't help but take on some of the things they have.

Consciously choose your friends, knowing that their interaction will have a profound effect on you.

That's what I did when I joined Toastmasters International. As I met with this positive, ambitious and dedicated group of people, I could tell that with exposure to them I would take on some of their attitudes and spirit. It's been twenty years, and I know I should have made more progress, but I attribute much of my success to the members of that great organization.

There are many other fine organizations you might want to affiliate yourself with, but take my word for it, Toastmasters International is one of the best.

■ *Love yourself*

"I'm a failure and I hate myself!" It was Gina, and we were reminiscing after six or seven years of not seeing each other. Gina was feeling sorry for herself and a little sad about the way things had turned out.

I tried to encourage her, but she continued to downgrade and criticise herself. Finally I said to her, "Gina, do you know what you should do?" She looked up expectantly. "Tonight when you go home, go to the mirror and look yourself straight in the eye and say out loud, I'm a beautiful person."

She seemed shocked at my suggestion. "Oh, I couldn't do that," she said. "I couldn't do that," she repeated. The thought of telling herself that she was a beautiful person seemed alien to her.

But she had no problem telling herself she was a failure, and she was ugly and she hated herself. She could tell herself that she was good for nothing. That was O.K.! But to tell herself she was beautiful, "Oh no!" She sounded even a little proud of the fact she was so critical of herself. As if that was the right thing to do, and to think of herself as beautiful was somehow wrong and immoral.

I took that opportunity to tell her how beautiful we all are. How much potential we all have to be great and successful and victorious. I told her of the emotions of love and harmony and peace that abide in all of us. I told her how wonderfully and magnificently we are made, and that every human being is a miracle. I told her The Creator didn't make ugly people, but we make ourselves ugly through the medium of choice. That there was nothing wrong with telling ourselves we are beautiful.

When we get to thinking we are beautiful and everybody else is ugly, that is where the immorality is. When we become so arrogant we think we know it all, and that everyone else is wrong and ignorant, that's where the real problem exists.

Brian Tracy, author/narrator of the **Psychology of Achievement** and one of America's best-known speakers, encourages his audiences to repeat again and again the words: "I like myself, I like myself, I like myself."

Do some things today to prove to yourself you like yourself. Write a letter to yourself. Send yourself a Christmas card or a birthday card. Give yourself a special gift, like a mug that says, "You are the greatest." Do something, anything, that says "I like myself and I'll take the time to show it."

■ Give yourself away

If your thoughts are for yourself alone, you won't get very far. If the only person you like is yourself, your world will be a very small place. Probably a dark and unhappy place too. But if liking yourself helps you to discover others and what you can do for them, you are on the right road. When you like yourself enough to know you have something to contribute, your confidence level will rise and good things will happen.

Your gifts and abilities were meant to be shared, so look for opportunities to give yourself away. Sometimes you may get paid for doing it, and other times you won't.

Rose Winters is a colleague of mine in the business of professional speaking. Rose told me she consciously and deliberately looks for opportunities where she can speak for free. She feels she owes it to the society that has done so much for her. The other side to Rose's experience is that she is so much in demand for paid speeches, she can hardly find time to do her free speeches. But she insists she must give away some of her gift. It's tempting to believe The Universe is taking care of Rose and making sure she gets a good return on her investment.

Years ago I thought I had nothing to give. When an executive position in our local Toastmasters' chapter became vacant, I never thought of applying. Fortunately, I was drafted. That happens often in Toastmasters.

It opened up a whole new world for me. I began to participate at business meetings and share my views with others. I became responsible for one aspect of running the organization. My confidence level rose and the next year I volunteered for more responsibilities. I had tasted the satisfaction and reward that comes from helping others. From there on there was no stopping me. I kept on giving myself away, and the return has been more than enough in both a material and spiritual sense.

There are hundreds of organizations in which you can get involved and serve others. You might like to start with the associations that serve your particular field. Then there are community service clubs that do an outstanding job in most communities. There are hospitals and seniors' homes and welcome wagons and youth organizations. The list is endless. These are opportunities where you can invest your time and talents and get a return of greater self-confidence and spiritual satisfaction.

■ *Take a risk*

Gloria was a quiet, shy and fearful young woman. I wondered how she had generated the courage to come to the workshop. She hardly raised her eyes during the introductory comments I made and seemed reluctant to participate in the morning's discussions. I wondered if she would get anything out of the workshop. Lunch time arrived and all the participants went out. I was alone in the room.

I was rather surprised when Gloria returned a good twenty minutes before the scheduled start time. She walked over to me with a determined look on her face. I could see she had something to tell me. I could see she was quite excited. I looked up and met her eyes. She was smiling. "I ordered a cup of coffee in the restaurant today," she said.

I waited. There had to be more. Surely, there had to be more. But there wasn't any more. You see Gloria had taken a risk, and she was proud of herself. She had never ordered a cup of coffee in a restaurant before. That day in the seminar something was said that inspired her to take a risk. And now she felt good about herself. She had grown in stature and in confidence. It was just a little thing, but for her it was a giant step forward in her struggle with her fears and emotions.

Maybe it doesn't bother you to ask for a cup of coffee in a restaurant. Maybe you need a bigger challenge than Gloria had. Wherever you are, you need to challenge yourself. You need to step out and take a risk.

Years ago when I was afraid to stand up and speak before an audience, I took the risk of entering a speech contest. I didn't do very well in my first, or indeed in my second contest. But I kept on taking that risk. Eventually, I started winning and reaping the rewards of increased confidence.

Everything in life is a risk. If you hide yourself away from every potential mistake or embarrassing moment, you will end up hiding away from life.

10 Ways to increase Self-Worth

- Take a look at yourself
- Beware of negative pictures
- Use your greatest gift
- Sow seeds of success
- Use synthetic experience
- Prepare your good list now
- Choose your friends carefully
- Love yourself
- Give yourself away
- Take a risk

Chapter 10

THE ART OF MANAGING SUCCESS

Questions, questions, questions

If I were to ask you to talk about the most successful person you knew, who would it be? What kind of person would your mind immediately focus on? Would you think of someone who had a lot of money? Or would your thoughts trend towards those who are in the spotlight in your city or town? What are the factors that add up to success? Who are the successful people today and yesterday and tomorrow?

Questions, questions, questions! They have been asked since time began, but still we keep asking, "What is success?"

My hero

When I was a little boy I knew a man who became my hero. He was a successful man. I thought of him as a giant among men, although in actual size he was quite a small man. I can't remember him ever being mentioned in the news, or on radio or television. He never moved with the rich and powerful people of the city in which I lived. But he had a rich circle of friends. Almost without exception they regarded him with love and affection. Among the people that formed his world, he was regarded with respect and even adoration. He was a fanatic for dependability and honesty. His business associates often said that they trusted him absolutely.

He was a cheerful man. He knew how to laugh and have fun, although his concept of fun was being at one end of a fishing line, and most times nothing at the other end. He had a streak of the sentimental in him. He would sometimes recite long poems he had learned in his youth - sad poems that made the tears run down his face, while we watched and listened, fascinated. He was a gentle man, but strong and firm in the principles in which he believed. He didn't bend for anyone when it came to honesty and integrity.

You probably have guessed by this that I am talking about my father. Was he a successful person? When he died I wrote a little piece about him that said: "......he lived a victorious life."

The worthwhile things are all free

It takes a long time to discover the worthwhile things are all free and they already belong to us. So many of us spend our lives wishing we could win the lottery, or some rich uncle would die and leave us great wealth or our business activities would result in financial success.

So few of us realize the things that really matter are already available and indeed have always belonged to us. We don't have to go out and buy them, we don't have to steal them or fight others to achieve them. They belong to us and are ready waiting to be used. What are they?

Priceless Possessions

Earl Nightingale in his award winning recording, **The strangest secret,** told us that the things that money can buy are not very valuable: "...the things that cost us money are actually very cheap and can be replaced at any time. A good man can be completely wiped out and make another fortune. He can do that several times. Even if our home burns down we can rebuild it. But the things we got for nothing, we can never replace."

Those irreplaceable things that Earl Nightingale told us about are the inner things, "......our minds, our souls, our bodies, our hopes, our dreams, our ambitions, our intelligence, our love of family and children and friends and country. All these priceless possessions are free."

Success

Success is when we finally come to the place where we begin to see what is worthwhile and valuable. That rich relationships and friendships are far more fulfilling and rewarding than the jingle of a jackpot in Las Vegas. That the love and respect of those around us - friends, family, peers and colleagues - is what comes first on the list for managing success.

The rest of the list is made up of the many strategies, secrets, ways and keys shared with you in the pages of this book. All 96 of them are closely related in that they reflect different facets of a central and eternal truth......"do unto others as you would have them do unto you."

The end

$29.95

SPEAK WITH CONFIDENCE
by Vince DaCosta
Three Cassettes(3 hours)

Quite often we close the door to opportunity because of fear of expressing our ideas. Thinking on your feet, or controlling your nervousness can be achieved through learning a few simple techinques. You too can chair committee meetings, make business presentations and give after dinner speeches. You too can raise your image and increase your visibility within your own company or community. These tapes will help you become an individual who can speak with authority before an audience of one or one thousand.

Add 7% G.S.T., $2.00 postage and mail cheque to:
Vince DaCosta & Associates Inc.
17 Ferrah St., Unionville, Ontario
L3R 1N4

$19.95

HOW TO MOTIVATE PEOPLE
by Vince Dacosta
Two Cassettes(1.5 hours)

The secret of motivation is to create a positive climate in which people motivate themselves. Given this creative environment, people will use their personal initiative and imagination in their approach to work. They will develop solutions to organizational and productivity problems. Generating this creative environment is what these tapes are all about.

Add 7% G.S.T., $2.00 postage and mail cheque to:
Vince Dacosta & Associates Inc.
17 Ferrah St., Unionville, Ontario.
L3R 1N4

$9.95

NEGOTIATION
The Win-Win Technique
by Vince DaCosta
One Cassette (45 minutes)

Whether you are striving to win a sales contract, settling an employer/employee problem or dealing with suppliers, you need negotiating skills to come out a winner. You must understand how to establish the right climate, handle conflict, generate options and use objective criteria. The secret is to forge an agreement that leaves both parties with a sense of having won. This tape details the strategies that maximize chances for success and provide reliable advice on avoiding the mistakes that characterize the poor negotiator.

Add 7% G.S.T., $1.00 postage and mail cheque to:
Vince DaCosta & Associates Inc.
17 Ferrah St., Unionville, Ontario.
L3R 1N4

$14.95

The Iacocca Formula
Time Management Techniques
How to Handle Difficult People
by Vince DaCosta..........LIVE!!
One Cassette (60 minutes)

85% of employees are relatively easy to manage. It's that other 15% that are a challenge - they are the difficult people!
On this tape, Vince DaCosta addresses this challenge of handling difficult people. Listen to him .....Live, as he speaks to an audience of managers and executives.